Ragdolls

By
Henry Golde

Published by:
Golde Publishing
2011 Regency Court
Appleton, WI 54915

For quantity discounts, contact the publisher.

Printed by:
PrintSource Plus
115 N. Mason
Appleton, WI 54914

Designer: PrintSource Plus
Typeface: Adobe Garamond

Manufactured in the United States of America

ISBN 0-9724213-0-0

5th Edition
First printing 2002

10 9 8 7 6 5 4 3 2 1

Dedicated to my whole family and to all my friends that encouraged me to finish this book.

Special thanks to Sally Johnson who edited and helped me to publish.

Contents

Preface	viii
Chapter I	1
Chapter II	5
Chapter III	19
Chapter IV	29
Chapter V	31
Chapter VI	39
Chapter VII	47
Chapter VIII	53
Chapter IX	63
Chapter X	69
Chapter XI	77
Chapter XII	97
Chapter XIII	111
Chapter XIV	121
Chapter XV	127
Chapter XVI	139
Chapter XVII	147
Chapter XVIII	159
Chapter XVIX	163
Epilogue	173

PREFACE

This is my story. When I was a boy, age eleven, I was taken and held prisoner for five years in nine different German concentration camps, six located in Poland, two in Germany and one in Czechoslovakia. These camps were noted as the worst prisons the world has ever seen. My only crime was that of being a Jew.

For five years, I faced death every moment of the day and night. My diet consisted of one piece of dry bread and a small portion of watery soup. Some days there was no food. I did not grow, not even an inch. For five years I didn't know what it was like to wear a pair of socks, underwear or a shirt, even in the bitterest of European winters. I was beaten and degraded by Nazi guards, anti-semitic polish sympathizers and Jewish police who were willing to treat their own people cruelly to save themselves. Along with other, I was reduced to an animal-like existence. Until this time, I was a normal fun-loving boy, happy with my family, enjoying sports, particularly soccer. My friends and I did all the things an average boy does. However, at the age of eleven, I became an adult. Five years later, I felt like an old man. I attribute my survival to a strong mind, self-respect, a will to live and probably some small miracles.

My beloved family, (Mother, Father, and sixteen-year-old brother, perished in 1941 during the first years of the Holocaust at Treblinka, along with many of my friends, neighbors and other Polish Jews.

CHAPTER I

At eleven, I was small for my age, thin with blonde hair and blue eyes, a quick wit, and a penchant for playing soccer along with a somewhat stubborn disposition. I was enjoying the days at our summer camp near the small town of Ciechanuw, approximately thirty kilometers from my hometown of Plock in Poland.

The camp was located in a clearing in the middle of a forest. Two barracks-type buildings were built on the mountain top in the forest. One of the buildings was sleeping quarters for fifty Jewish children, the other served as the dining hall with additional housing for our supervisor and her family. Only Jewish children who attended the Jewish school in Plock could attend this summer retreat.

The entire camp was surrounded by the forest, tall pines with long lacy needles. A narrow dirt road led to the main road, which was also dirt, but much wider. This was the road that led to Plock. I loved the camp, the peacefulness of living in the midst of nature, the serenity of the pines. The forest also gave us relief from the summer heat. Looking down the mountain, I could see the small clear lake. Surely this must be the most beautiful place on earth, I thought. A small stream spilled out over a ledge into the lake making a natural cascade of water for campers to shower. We picked mushrooms and berries sometimes, and played soccer and other games to our hearts' content. My friends and I liked soccer most of all.

In front of our campgrounds was a well-kept lawn with a flagpole. Every morning the Polish flag was raised while we stood at attention and sang the Polish national anthem. In the evening, the flag was lowered in accordance to patriotic customs.

Then one day, Rotman, the driver of the lorry, drove into camp.

"Quickly," he said to the supervisor, "Quickly, have the children gather their things and get into the lorry."
I listened while he continued telling one of the teachers that the parents had paid him to come and get us.

"War is imminent," he spoke rapidly. "The government has requisitioned my lorry. We must hurry."

After gathering our belongings, we were quickly loaded on the lorry. I took a long look around and wondered if I would ever see this camp again. To me, it was heaven itself. Surely, I would return.

The lorry rumbled down the bumpy dirt road. I began thinking about the rumors of war. All I knew of war was what my father had told me about his service in the Revolution. He served in the Russian Czarist Army because, at that time, Plock and the surrounding area was overrun with Russians. The Russians didn't care who was Polish or who was Russian. They simply took all the young men. Father spoke solemnly of the war and the horrors it held for him. Still, in my eleven-year-old mind, there was forbidden excitement, romance in fighting or being in the army, and I wished I were older so I could go to war.

Tension mounted as we drove into town. Rotman took a few detours on the way to the Market Square.

"Your parents will come to pick you up there." He told us. Driving into town, I watched the stone houses go by. Linden trees lined the cobbled streets. People were digging big holes in the street and placing steel bars in them. Later, I learned those 'traps' were designed to stop the German tanks.

When we arrived at Market Square, a small crowd of parents and friends greeted us. Mother grabbed me, held me and kissed me.

"Mother, not in front of all these people," I told her.

I was home, back in Plock. The town I was born in, the town I lived in, the town I loved. Plock was a successful, flourishing town of twenty thousand people and lay approximately a hundred kilometers north of Warsaw. It was situated at the top of a mountain; at the bottom flowed the Vistula River. Along the edge of the mountain was Tumy, a lovely park that stretched for miles. Rising above all else in the center of Tumy was an enormous cathedral. The inhabitants of Plock liked parks, hence, we had five. Plock was often referred to as "The City of Parks." Two bridges crossed the river connecting the suburb of Ragiwic to the economic, cultural, and educational facilities of Plock.

We turned on Sheroka Ulica, which is a very wide street, wide enough to have a boulevard. Most of the two thousand Jews who lived in Plock lived in this area. Old story tellers would tell us, "Many years ago, Sheroka was a Jewish ghetto." My family lived on Krulewicka Ulica. My father also had his barber shop on the same street. Adjacent to Krulewicka was the Market Square.

Farmers came from miles around every Tuesday and Friday. In the center of Market Square was a huge round building with cubicles. Butchers displayed their meats and sausages in these cubicles. Farm produce was exhibited in the center of the area. Housewives came to barter for goods, con artists tried to cheat the farmers of their money and, as everyone visited back and forth, the noise level grew louder with each passing hour. My eyes and ears could not take it all in.

One incident I remember was the time Mrs. Ruebens went to the butcher in the first stall. She examined each piece of meat, touching each as she went.

"What can I do for you?" asked the butcher while sharpening his knife.

"What? You call that meat? It looks more like a dead horse to me!" Mrs. Ruebens complained.

Sharpening his knife a little faster, the butcher retorted, "If you don't like it, go next door. After you touch every piece of meat in the market you will still come back and buy mine for I have the best."

"HA! If you have the last piece of meat in the market, I will never come back to you," she retorted. With that remark she left his stall and moved on to the next.

Meanwhile, a con man was haggling with a farmer over the price of a sack of potatoes and arguing for free delivery. He convinced the farmer to deliver, evading mention that his apartment was on the third floor. The farmer drove his cart to the address, a few blocks away from the square. He climbed down from the cart, threw the sack of potatoes over his shoulder and huffed and puffed as he climbed three flights of stairs. He was then greeted by a surly voice from inside.

"We ordered no potatoes. Get out of here."
Returning to his cart, the farmer found that both his horses and his cart were missing.

"Help. Help!" he called out. The poor farmer tried to explain his predicament to the police. I felt very sorry for him.

Father was also busy on market day. In spite of the fact that he was a barber, many people depended on him to diagnose and treat their ailments. Sometimes, he even pulled teeth for those in dire need.

Making our way through the clamor and crowds of the Market Square, Mother and I hastened to our apartment where neighbors and friends were talking excitedly about the possibility of war.

CHAPTER II

That night, we sat in the living room listening to the radio. The government was calling for a general mobilization and all men between the ages of 18 and 45 were called to serve. The next day father and his employees were ordered to the army barracks, one of which was the Calvary, the second the Artillery. Remembering parades of the past, those given during national holidays and special occasions, my imagination began to run wild. The men in their uniforms with lances looked handsome and strong, the horses fitted out with fancy harnesses, saddles and braids looked spectacular. People cheered them for they were the defenders of our country. We all felt safe, content and secure. There was no doubt in anybody's mind that when war broke out those same soldiers would fight and win again. They wouldn't allow any foreign army to set foot on the soil of Poland.

My brother, Marcus, along with the other young men, ages 16 to 18, were told to report to the Home Guard at Jagelonka High School for future training. They were issued uniforms and rifles. Temporary quarters with cots and a kitchen had been set up. All the young men were confined to the temporary barracks until further notice. Plock had only one siren. It was moved and placed on the roof of the Jagelonka High School and the Home Guard was charged with maintaining it.

Proclamations were posted on street corners directing civilians to report for work digging ditches, filling sacks with dirt for gun placements. So many holes were dug into the streets that it looked like rodents had burrowed through. The town was busy, people were rushing here and there preparing for the war, the excitement was mounting. War was the main topic of conversation! Neighbors without radios arrived to listen for the latest news. We even listened to Hitler's speeches in spite of the fact that no one could understand German. We thought he sounded like a raving maniac.

Dad came home after spending two days and nights working straight through. "I'm so tired."

"I'm so glad you're home," said Mother as she ran to him. "I have been worried sick about you," she said while hugging Dad. "And where is Marcus? Is he with you? When will he be home? Will they send him to fight? He is only a baby."

"Don't worry, Gina," Dad said, "they will not let him go to war. They have more than enough men to beat Hitler."

"If he gets home, I won't let him go back. I will burn the uniform he is wearing. I'll not let my son be killed, not for a country that doesn't give a damn about the Jews."

"Shhh! Shhh! Shhh! Shhh! Don't worry so. He'll not go to fight."

They began to argue, Mom fretting, Dad defending and reassuring. But the last word was Dad's.

"It's late! Time to go to bed."

I couldn't sleep. With my eyes closed I could see the great Polish army, the courageous men in their beautiful uniforms. I pictured them on their horses parading in front of the townspeople. And Marcus would be the tallest, the bravest, the most handsome of all the soldiers. I could picture him bravely fighting the Germans. When he came home, his chest would be covered with medals for valor. He would be a hero.

I woke with a start, sweating at the onset of another hot summer's day. I looked to the east and saw the rising sun. Mom was rattling pots and pans about in the kitchen as she busied herself cooking breakfast, but somehow I knew Dad had already left. Sleepily, I walked into the kitchen.

"Sit down and eat, Henry," Mom directed.

I didn't want to eat; I wanted to go out into the street to see what had happened over the night and what was happening now. Gulping my food, I left the table and ran out through the courtyard and down the street to Dad's barbershop.

My father was busy cutting a customer's hair; the second barber was giving old Mr. Dombrowski a shave and the third barber was sitting in his chair reading a newspaper.

"What's happening? Did the army leave yet? Did the war start yet?," I asked.

"Henry, settle down," answered Dad. "The army left in the middle of the night. The war has not started yet."

I was disappointed that I had not seen the soldiers marching out. Thinking I might find Marcus, I walked over to the high school. A sentry stood in front of the school carrying a rifle over his shoulder. He kept an eye on the wood picket fence that ran around the high school. I craned my neck, then I tried jumping, but the fence surrounding the courtyard was too high. I tried to find a hole, a crack anywhere so I could see what was going on. I heard someone giving orders to another person inside the fence. Then the sentry saw me. He walked over to where I was standing.

"Beat it, kid!"

Walking back through town, I noticed that people were still digging holes in the road. That's stupid, I thought, if the Germans can't come down Main Street, they'll just go a block over. Turning onto our street, I saw the Dombrowskis digging a hole in our backyard.

"What are you doing?" I asked.

"Don't ask questions, start helping us." I grabbed a gunny sack and started to fill it with dirt.

"We're building a bomb shelter," they replied.

"A bomb shelter," I asked, "what for?"

"Don't ask stupid questions. Keep working."

I wondered about this hole in the ground. Is this going to stop a bomb? Nothing is making sense to me. The holes in the streets to stop tanks, the holes in the ground for bomb shelters. If everyone thinks our Army will stop the Germans, why do me need these holes? On the other hand, who knew? The German border was only eighty kilometers from Plock. That wasn't very far. But I kept working anyway.

Towards the end of the day, the shelter was done. They put some tin over the hole. What for, I asked myself, that piece of tin isn't going to stop the bombs. I didn't think too much of the shelter. I decided that if the bombing did start, I wouldn't get into that hole.

It was almost five in the afternoon, time for supper so I headed home. Dad was sitting in the living room, twisting the radio dial in hopes of hearing the latest news.

"Have you heard anything," I asked.

"No!"

Mom called us to the table. We listened, but all we could hear were patriotic songs. The announcer introduced Marshall Ridz-Smigly who had taken over as Poland's leader when Marshall Pilsudski died. His speech was long, very long.

"The glorious Polish army will crush and invaders that dare to come on Polish soil. Everyone must contribute in every possible way for the upcoming struggles." He droned on and on saying the same thing over and over. We listened closely. When he was done talking, they played the National Anthem. It was hard to get to sleep that night. I couldn't wait to know what would happen.

The next morning I was up, out of bed and back on the street again. Close to noon there was a loud roar in the sky. People stood there on the street, shading their eyes, staring upward and saying, "Those are our planes." Two planes roared over town flying so fast that you barely caught them in eyesight before they were gone again. The noise got louder as the planes, bearing the German black Iron Cross flew over Plock. Seconds later, there was a big explosion. Houses trembled and shook; then another explosion. After that, stillness. Suddenly people began to panic, running every which way as they realized the planes were German. I, too, was excited and ran to Dad's barbershop. Everyone in the shop was talking:

"Those are German planes!"

"They dropped bombs on the army barracks!"

"They might come back!"

"They might not come back," said Dad, trying to calm everyone. "War hasn't been declared yet. Let's listen to the radio." Dad turned the radio on. All that could be heard was music. "See, there is nothing to worry about. They wouldn't be playing music if war had been declared."

"Two bombs just fell on the Army barracks," said a man who walked in off the street, "but no one was hurt because the army had gone."

A voice on the radio interrupted the music, "A number of Polish cities have been bombed by the German Luftwaffe. Poland has declared war on Germany."

Everyone sat still, stunned and unable to speak. Then suddenly everyone spoke at once. The town siren cut through the babble with its shrill blast.

"Why didn't the sirens sound before the planes came?" someone wondered aloud. I silently agreed with him.

Yet two hours later, things had settled back down and people were tending to business as usual. But, not for long! A large group of planes thundered through the sky. This time the siren blew loud and clear, warning people to take cover. Men, women and children scattered in all directions seeking shelter. My friends and I stood outside watching the planes come closer. The airplanes loomed large and threatening in the sky. As they disappeared from view, the sirens faded and people ventured back out into the street. Grownups came out of the shelter that I had helped build yesterday. I was glad to see them safe.

Mom came out of our apartment house. She was crying. Catching sight of me, she came over to me and scolded, "How dare you stand out here in the open scaring me half to death. I didn't know where you were, if you were alive or what." She shook me by the shoulders and just as fast as she had started to shout, she let go. She turned to go to the barbershop to check on Dad. "And you go straight home, " she called over her shoulder.

But I didn't. I went with her.

"Oh Felix," she cried, "you're all right. Where were you during the air raid?"

"I was standing here by the window," Dad said.

The announcer's voice came from the radio: "Warsaw has been attacked by air. The damage to our capitol is extensive. There are many casualties."

That was where the planes had gone, to Warsaw. Yet, once again, life settled back into its usual routine.

I awoke the next day hearing the radio blaring. Dad had turned it on very loud. The latest news came over the airwaves: "The Polish front at Muwava has been broken by the Germans. The Polish army is trying to regroup."

"Where is Marcus? Why haven't we heard from him?" asked Mom as she paced the floor.

"I'll go look for him. I'll try the high school first," I volunteered.

The guard outside the high school was having a bad time of it. A crowd of people were pushing up close to him, asking about their sons.

"Will someone come out here and give me a hand?" the guard called out. An older man appeared.

"Your sons are all fine, but no one is allowed inside the building," he said. Then, he turned around and went back inside. The people grumbled, but they started to disband.

I found new excitement, walking downtown. Soldiers were marching through town, mostly in small groups of two. Their uniforms were torn and dirty. They made their way towards the bridge on their way to Warsaw. A horse and cart came by loaded with wounded soldiers and then more soldiers on foot. They looked downtrodden, glum and beaten. People tried to talk to them, asked them all kinds of questions, but none of the soldiers would answer. More and more kept coming, most looked like they would collapse any minute. Many looked as if they had not slept for days. Where are the beautiful horses the soldiers rode when they left for front, I thought, what could have happened to them?

Making my way back to Dad's barbershop, I overheard many things grownups were saying.

"The Polish army is regrouping and forming a front line right here in Plock."

"The Germans are just a few miles away."

"What shall we do?"

"We'll all die!"

Dad's barbershop was full of people listening to the radio and taking all at once.

"We should leave and go to Warsaw because Warsaw will be defended," someone said.

"But if we go there, we'll be caught in the middle of the war," Dad told them.

I left to go home. I wanted to be the one to tell Mom what I had seen and heard both at the high school and in the streets.

Mom started to cry. "What's going to happen to us? I tried to comfort her as best as I could, but she was still crying when Dad came home. He looked troubled, but Mom stopped crying when she saw him. While she was putting supper on the table, Marcus walked in. Mom ran to him, hugged and kissed him. I, too, went to Marcus. I patted him on the back.

"I am glad to see you," Dad said, tearfully, "sit down and eat." "I only have half an hour to say goodbye. I'm going to the front tonight. Lots of people are leaving town, going across the river toward Warsaw," said Marcus.

Dad was very quiet. After taking time for thought, he spoke, "Take off that uniform, Marcus. You're not going back. We are going to Warsaw with the others." Marcus didn't need much persuasion. I don't think he really wanted to fight.

"What will we do with the uniform?" he asked. "Let's hide it."

"No, someone will find it," Dad said.

"Let's burn it."

"NO! We have no time for that. We have to leave as soon as possible." Dad turned to me. "Henry, you go bury the uniform." While I was busy doing that, Mom packed some essentials into a knapsack. Within an hour we were on our way.

"If anyone stops us and asks about Marcus, we will say he is only fifteen," Mom instructed us.

We made our way to the downtown area joining crowds of people crossing the bridge, hoping to get to Warsaw where they thought they would be safe. A steady stream of soldiers were headed in the same direction. We held our breath, hoping not to be stopped. If they found out Marcus was supposed to be in the Home Guard, he would be shot of the spot. We walked shoulder to shoulder with men, women, children, horses, soldiers and ox carts in a somber silence.

"Keep moving! They are going to blow up the bridge," someone said.

But for the most part, the long line of humanity continued to walk quietly, tiredly, toward their destination. I was disappointed, I remembered the speeches given just a few days ago. Where are all these people going, I wondered. What is the sense in this? Are we all running away from the fighting? NO, we are just prolonging the agony. What happened to " We won't give an inch of our Polish soil" to anyone? Our glorious army doesn't look so glorious anymore. These are the soldiers that are going to defend Warsaw? Where are their rifles? They probably threw them away. They can hardly walk. How are they going to fight? NO! NO! Everything is lost. These were my thoughts, the words I said to myself as I walked the dusty dirt road to Warsaw.

We made it across the Vistula River without incidents and onto the highway. It was so dark on the road. Tall dark forests stood along both sides of the highway. A sign read 100 kilometers to Warsaw.

"Are we going to walk all that way?" I grouched. "My feet are already sore and I'm tired. Can't we sit down for awhile?"

"Keep walking," Dad said, "and don't talk. If you talk while you walk, you will get more tired."

I thought he was right. Dad was usually right. But I worried about how far I could walk. What if I couldn't walk anymore? I would slow everybody down. Then the Germans would catch us. Would they shoot us?"

The moon came out from behind the clouds. As far as I could see ahead of us and as far as I could see behind us, there were people walking in the same direction. Everybody, soldiers, civilians, horses walked with their heads down, as if they were half asleep. How far were we, I wondered. We'd walked for hours. I was so tired. I wanted to lie down and go to sleep. But I had to keep up. I had to keep walking.

"Are you tired Henry," asked Marcus.

"I'm so tired I think I'm dead," I answered.

"Jump on my back. I'll carry you for a bit," he suggested. It felt good to be carried. The blisters on my feet burned and stung. I noticed Dad supporting Mother. I realized she must be very tired, too.

"Put me down Marcus. I can walk now." After he put me down, I looked up at him. He was so tall. And strong, too. I felt very small next to him.

"There is a cart in front of us with soldiers lying in the back. They are covered with blankets. Jump on the back, they are sleeping. They won't mind if you ride with them," said Dad. I was tired. I lay down of top of someone and fell asleep. I didn't remember how long I slept, but when I woke I realized that not once had the soldier moved. It was then I knew that the soldier was dead. I leaped off the cart.

"Marcus, those soldiers in that cart. I think they are all dead. I was sleeping on top of them!" I walked, I walked faster than I had ever walked before, but I could not shake the idea that I had slept on top of dead people.

The sky was lightening as the sun peeked over the horizon. Still we walked. Five miles to Gombin a sign informed us.

"Gombin is a small resort town with a beautiful forested area," Dad told us. "My family came here many times for summer holidays when times were better. When we get to Gombin, we will stop and take a rest." I nodded my head in agreement.

The village was overwhelmed to see so many people all at once. Most of the people kept on walking, but some decided to stay. We sat in the grass near the village square and ate lunch, although it was really breakfast. Mom had packed some bread and sausage and the nourishment gave us a fresh outlook on things.

"We must make a decision. Are we going to stay here or go on to Warsaw?" Dad asked.

Mom spoke, "I don't want to go to Warsaw."

"All right then. We'll stay here. I know a barber here in the village. I'll go see him and find out if he knows of some lodging for us."

After a short period of time, Dad returned. "Shhh! Don't say a word. Just follow me. There are many people who would give anything to find a place to stay. There is an empty house on the other side of the village. If we find it and if no one else is there, we can stay."

While walking to the house we met people who had lived above us, a young man, his wife, his aging mother and their two-year-old daughter. They were Catholic and before the bombings they would never speak to us. Now it was a different story.

"We can't find any place to stay," he said crying.

"Come along," Dad invited. He felt sorry for them, especially the baby.

After finding the house, Dad went to the Polish farmer. "Will you let us stay there?"

"Yes," agreed the farmer.

It was a large piece of land with an apple orchard in the back. The house was white with a black roof and consisted of three bare rooms. There wasn't even a stove to cook on. The farmer gave us some straw. We took one corner in the middle room and our neighbors took the opposite corner in the same room.

When we ran out of food, Dad walked into the village to buy some. There was none to be had. All the people who had come through town had bought everything. Dad went back to talk with the farmer.

"Will you sell us some food?"

"I don't know that I should," he replied. "Perhaps I could get into trouble. Perhaps I would run out of food myself. What would I do then?" Finally, he caved in and we had some black pumpernickel bread and a slice of butter. Not much, but better that nothing.

From a distance, we could hear artillery fire getting closer and closer. Towards evening the shells were whistling by. Some hit houses in the village. We were grateful for the quiet of the night. Since there was no electricity or candles in the house, we sat in the dark talking and wondering how the Germans would treat the Polish people. There were rumors of atrocities against the Czechoslovakians and the Jews, especially the Jews.

"Bah, "said Dad. "I fought against the Germans in the first world war. They are not that bad."

The straw on the floor did not make a comfortable bed. Nevertheless, I fell asleep quickly.

Next morning was horribly noisy. Shells whistled by and the explosions were very close at hand. I wanted to go outside.

"No Henry," said Mom. "you stay right here."

"Mom, I have to go to the bathroom," I said.

"Okay, but come right back," she answered me, sighing.

I ran to the orchard. Whistle, bang, whistle. I was very scared. What would happen if I got hit with one of the shells when my pants were down? I finished by business and ran back to the house.

My heart pounded for all I was worth. Everyone was scared, not just me.

Suddenly we heard the droning of airplanes. They were getting closer and closer and closer. Soon, the bombs were dropping. The air was filled with explosions all around us. The baby started to cry, the women started praying. I wanted to go to the window and watch. Dad pulled me to the floor.

"Stay away from the windows. If they shattered, your face would get cut up," he said.

It seemed an eternity that the bombs rained down on us. Then a peculiar silence came. We got up to look out the window. Trees in the orchards had fallen over, others were uprooted and some stood untouched. Then the heavy droning of the planes returning sent us back to the floor. We huddled in a corner, both families together.

"Maybe we should go out into the orchard," our neighbor suggested.

"No. Then the pilots would see us. We'd better stay inside," Marcus said.

"We'll all die," Mom cried.

I thought so, too. Tears ran down my face. I looked at the others. Marcus was chewing his bottom lip, Mom and the neighbor's wife were crying. The neighbor was biting his fingernails while his wife rocked the baby back and forth. Only Dad looked the same, quiet, somber and calm. While the bombs fell, we put our arms around each other; we turned our faces away burying them in each others' bodies seeking comfort.

The next explosion was so close that the window shattered, showering us with glass. Luckily, there were only a few minor scratches and a few small shards sticking to our clothing. Another quiet spell settled in. Then from the west came the familiar sound of the Blitz Krieg. They flew over us dropping bombs everywhere. They came in waves of twenty, thirty airplanes at a time, and bombed us again and again all day long.

We hadn't eaten the entire day. We were scared, tired, worried and hungry. When we no longer heard the planes and thought we were safe, we walked across the street to the farmer's house. The damage done by the bombs was immense. There were holes in the ground and piles of rubble that used to be buildings. Strangely, the farmer's house stood in the middle of the ruins untouched. Not one single bomb had come close to the house. He and his entire family were huddled in the kitchen, still frightened by the day's torturous events.

"We will not spend another day like this one. We are going into the forest to hide. It will be safer there. Why don't you come with us," suggested the farmer. The adults talked it over but decided to take our chances staying at the farmer's house.

"No!" said Dad, "we'll stay here but do you have some food? We haven't had anything to eat all day."

"Mama!" shouted the farmer. "Pack some food for us to take and set out some food for these poor people."

"We'll be happy to fix our own," Mom offered.

"Okay. But look after our farm while we are gone."

Mom and the neighbor's wife rummaged through the pantry and found some salt pork and potatoes. I discovered that when you are hungry, you will eat anything. But not Mom! She refused to eat any food that was not in keeping with her religion. It was not so with the rest of us. Dad, Marcus and I ate much like the animal the salt pork came from.

After we ate, we decided to go back to the farmhouse we had been staying in. Drained by the day's experience, and with our bellies full, it was easy to go to sleep.

The Blitz Kreig went on for the next two days. Dozens of airplanes flew over at a time. One group would barely leave our sight before the next squadron soared over us. The sky looked dark with huge planes bearing the black Iron Cross while dropping bombs like the leavings of pigeons. We were afraid to stay, and afraid to go. We were afraid of what would happen next.

On the third day, I heard birds chirping. Looking out the window, I could see a clear blue sky with a brilliant sun beaming down on us. What a beautiful morning. The heavens were quiet! No bombs! We decided to walk over to the farmer's house. His house had miraculously escaped the bombing. Just as we arrived, he and his family returned from the forest.

"Ach!" said the farmer. " We spent two days and two nights in the woods. We were afraid to lift our heads off the ground. I think you were smart to stay here. At least you had a roof over your heads."

"Yes," Dad agreed. "But it was bad. The bombs kept coming. I thought we would all die."

"Yes, I thought that, too. I cannot believe my house is still here. I was sure it would be gone."

"We must pay you for the food we have taken from your pantry," said Dad.

"No, I am happy to be alive," said the farmer. "I am happy to see you alive and you have taken care of my house. I'll not take money from you."

The grownups continued to talk among themselves, but when noon time came, our two families had decided to go back to Plock. While walking through the village of Gombin, one could easily see the toll that the bombings had taken. Beautiful houses, churches, and stores were destroyed. Everything was trashed. Townspeople were searching through the wreckage trying to find food, some momento of their past, some remnant of their lives before the bombing had occurred. It was sad. I didn't think war was glorious anymore.

CHAPTER III

The road leading backs to Plock was jammed with hundreds of people. We had lost the battle, but there was no sight of the enemy. We stopped to rest every now and then; we weren't in a hurry to get back. We were pensive, worried about what condition Plock would be in. Was Plock bombed out like Gombin?

The neighbor accompanied us on the way back home. We talked back and forth as though we had been friends for a long time. Now we had a common bond: we had survived the bombings, we had shared hunger and the deprivations of war. Would they forget we were Jews? Would they stay our friends?

A disturbance arose down the line. Murmuring noises became shouts.

"Move aside. The Germans are coming through!" someone called out. And come through they did. Troop after troop after troop. It seemed as though there was no end to the succession of German soldiers as they came marching down the middle of the road. I sucked in my breath. They looked so sharp with their rifles over their shoulders, their uniforms pressed and clean, every soldier in step with the next. Powerful! But, other than the color, the uniforms weren't that much different than the Polish Army uniforms. Maybe the rumors about their mannerisms, their superiority and their cruelty weren't true. I craned my neck to see the waves of soldiers parading by. At the end of the line came the staff cars. Each one had a German flag at both sides of their vehicle. The officers' uniforms were much fancier and every officer had a pair of binoculars around his neck.

Later the next day, we came to the town of Radziwide. There were no signs of war; everything stood as it was when we left. The war had not touched this village, but both bridges that crossed the Vistula River had been bombed. There was an empty gap where the bridges once stood.

"How will be get home?" asked Mom

"Stay here! I'll go see what is going on," Dad replied. In a short time he was back with good news.

"Come on! There are some boats that will ferry us across."

Two huge barges were on shore loading pedestrians from the south side carrying them over to the opposite shore of Plock. We stood in line for over an hour until it was our turn to board the boats. Every boat was loaded beyong its normal capacity. Two men rowed the boat, one in the bow and one in the stern. I watched closely as the barge slipped through the water. I thought we would tip over and all go drifting down the river. Mom, ever concerned about the cost of things, asked

"Did you have to pay very much to get us back to Plock?"

"Not very much, answered Dad.

I'm happy to be going back home. I'm happy things are going to be normal again."

We all were happy, but when we disembarked we found it very difficult to walk up the steep hill. We were all tired. Who wasn't? Everything looked the same. The holes in the road were untouched; houses stood where they had always been completely intact. Even the bomb shelter stood in the same condition as it had been when we left. Friends and neighbors stopped to visit. Stores were open for business and, most wondrous of all, no one had entered our apartment. Everything was in the same place as we left it. It seemed as though we had gone for a long walk, as though we had had a bad dream and woke up finding our lives in the same perfect rhythm as before. It was bizarre to think we had left town to avoid the war, gone through such extensive bombings only to return and find that Plock had given up without having fired one single shot.

However, when we reached the Market Square, we say Germans everywhere. Artillery guns drawn by special vehicles, tanks, many tanks, huge tanks! So much steel! How could the holes we dug ever stop one of those? There were trucks, motorcycles, bicycles and German soldiers everywhere.

"Oh, Felix," Mom said. "Look at all the Germans. What can this mean?"

"It means business," said Dad. "And I'm afraid it won't be good business."

It was hard to understand that if there had been no war, what were all the Germans doing here? We listened to the radio in hopes of learning the latest news. A few days later the news came over the airwave: "France and England have declared war on Germany."

We were elated. Even I, at the age of eleven, was overjoyed. The Germans wouldn't be here long. Those two big countries would come to our rescue. The next news we heard was that Russia had attacked Poland from the east. Without any hardships, they recovered a large portion of land back from the Poles. Excitement was in the air; the enemy would not be on our soil much longer. More news came: Warsaw is being defended. And later still we learned that Warsaw fell to the Germans and the Polish government had capitulated. The war was over. We had lost. The radio went quiet and there was no more news.

With the end of the war came changes, many changes. The field army marched through town. We noticed different uniforms: light blue uniforms were worn by the field police, yellow uniforms were worn by the S.A., and the black uniforms, with the skull and cross-bone insignia, were worn by the SS, the elite army of Hitler.

Slowly, quietly, we heard of arrests. At first most of them centered on the more prominent citizens of Plock: the Mayor, the judges, the principal of the high school and other influential citizens. They were gone, missing and never heard of again. Schools were no longer open to educate the young, radios were confiscated and the newspaper presses were no longer in operation.

Rumors ran wild. The gossip that affected us the most was that concerning the Jews. It was said that Jews were being taken to concentration camps and used for slave labor. Dad decided to go to Russia.

"I'll see if I can find a safe place for us there. Surely the Russians will give us a home. Marcus, you come with me!"

They hired an ox and cart from a neighbor and Mom packed

enough provisions to last the length of the trip.

"Henry, you must take care of Mother. You are the man of the house."

"Don't worry, Dad. I'll take good care of her." I was so proud that he gave me such great responsibility that I didn't even cry when they left.

Time was passing and I was learning German. Jewish people who spoke Yiddish (a lower form of Hebrew) were able to understand the German language better than the rest of us. Mom and Dad spoke Yiddish, but only when they didn't want Marcus or me to understand what was going on.

The Germans had expanded their position in town. They now had two full barracks of SS soldiers. Every day they marched through town singing German marching songs. Every day new laws were posted and every law that was broken carried the death penalty. Ration cards were issued. Christians were allowed more rations than Jews. Furthermore, Jews were only allowed to buy their grocery supplies at one store. All other stores were declared off limits. If a Jew was caught in another store, he or she would be executed right there.

More demands. Every Jew had to register with the authorities. Failure to comply was punishable by death. Then it was decided that Jews would be labeled. Every man, woman and child was ordered to wear a round circle of yellow material with the word 'Jew' printed, in black ink, in the middle. One patch was to be worn over the left breast, the other patch was to be worn in the center of the back. Jewish stores were closed; any existing merchandise was shipped to a German store.

While Dad was gone, two of his employees took over the management of the barbershop and gave Mom a percentage of the earnings so we had enough money to live on. Now I was the one that did most of the shopping. Mom was a homebody as were most women then. They tended to the housework, child care and baking. In their spare time, they visited with one another.

Now Dad's barbershop was closed. We salvaged very little from the shop, one chair, one mirror and a few tools for cutting hair. One of Dad's employees began to cut hair in the kitchen of our apartment.

In the beginning, the rations were quite generous. We were able to live in much the same manner we always had lived. We had plenty of bread, butter, sugar, flour and soap. But, slowly the rations were cut. Soap was one of the first things to be scarce, then sugar. As winter approached, we found ourselves scrimping along on about half of what we had in the beginning. I was no longer a finicky eater. I ate everything I could safely eat.

Marcus and Dad returned from Russia with bad news. The Russian border was closed.

"Is there no place for us to go?" asked Mom.

"No, Gina, the Germans are everywhere."

"What will we do?"

"The same as everyone else, my dear. We simply will have to endure and survive however we can." That turned out to be much easier said than done.

Another new law was passed. Whenever a Jew met a German soldier on the street, the Jew must show respect for the German uniform by stepping into the gutter and allowing the German to pass. It was dangerous for a Jew to be out and alone on the streets. It they caught a Jew alone, they beat him. I often went out in the evening to meet Dad. We had carefully arranged signals. If I saw any sign of a German, I would raise my hand to my head, as if brushing the hair out of my eyes. Then Dad was to duck into a doorway to avoid being seen. This system worked out very well until one night when a drunken SS officer staggered out of a tavern and came between Dad and me.

"Come here you dirty Jew," he shouted at Dad. I kept on walking, but Dad turned around to face the officer.

"Jew! I said come here!"

Dad stepped into the gutter, stood face to face with the officer and bowed in accordance with the law. The officer slapped Dad in the face, again and again and again. I saw Dad's body stiffen to ward off the blows.

"Get down on your Knees." Dad followed orders. To do anything else was to get the death penalty.

"Now, kiss my boots Jew."

Without a moment's hesitation, Dad bent over and kissed his

boots. At that moment the tavern owner came out. He was a very nice man in spite of the fact that he was a German National, a German by birth who wore a special band around his cuff to denote his German heritage.

"Come inside," he said. "Let this poor man go home to his family."

"All Jews are scum! They don't deserve to be treated any better than an animal."

"That may be true, but why bother yourself. Come back inside. I'll buy you another drink."

I had ducked into a doorway and stood there watching. Two friends were hiding in the same doorway with me. I was so lost, so frustrated. I wanted to run to Dad. I wanted to help him, but the other boys stopped me.

"Don't be a fool," they said. "You'll be killed."

"I don't care. Look what they are doing to him."

The officer looked at the tavern owner.

"Yah! I think another drink would be fine." Then he turned and kicked Dad in the ribs. Tears streamed down my face. Dad looked so little, so helpless. I sensed that Dad would never be the same again; he had been humiliated and beaten to a point of no return. I knew, somehow, that from this point forward he would never have the same steadfastness, the same sure way of handling things or the same self confidence. The Dad I had known was now gone.

Crying, I helped Father get on his feet. He leaned heavily on me as we walked home together. I blamed myself for what had happened. Yet, I knew in my heart it was bound to happen sooner or later. Supper time was sad that night. I couldn't eat. Father tried to console me, but I was past consolation.

Twenty families arrived from Germany. They told us more stories of concentration camps, how Nazi's stripped them of their belongings, how all Jews living in Germany were to be shipped to Poland. Another new law stated that all Jews must move to Sheroka Ulica. Many German Nationals took it upon themselves to enter Jewish homes and take whatever they wanted: silver, dishes, fur coats, furniture, anything. No one could, or would, stop them. We, too, were forced to move and after the German Nationals went through our apartment we were left with a few chairs, a small table and the bed my parents had slept in. Now all four of us slept in the same bed.

More new laws. All Jews would live in one room no matter how many in the family. No Jew was allowed to leave the area. Of course, these edicts, like al the others before, were punishable by death if not obeyed.

The Jews formed their own government in hopes of gaining some semblance of humanity. They created a Jewish Police force. They carried no guns and wore special hats and armbands with the words 'Jewish Police' written on them. They didn't have guns, but they carried thick wooden clubs.

The Jewish government opened a soup kitchen. However, I was still doing the grocery shopping and was able to get into the non-Jewish stores. I had refused to wear the Jew insignia and luckily I could pass for a non-Jew. I would walk into a German store, click my heels and salute saying "Heil Hitler." The clerk asked me what I needed, filled my order and then turned and thanked me. I was free to go. It was that easy. So, for quite some time I was able to get sugar, butter and many other necessities without getting caught. I could even get into the dairy store which meant I was able to get milk for some of the babies and little children. Until one bad day.

I was standing in line for milk with a container to be filled. A German woman in a white coat was ladling out the milk. As I drew close, I heard a woman in back of me talking.

"There is a Jew in front of us. The Jews don't deserve any milk."

I knew she was talking about me, but I was the very next in line to get milk. Since the woman was talking in Polish and the clerk was German, I didn't think I would be caught. The German clerk started pouring milk into my container. Suddenly a Polish woman from the back of the room dashed forward yelling, pointing at me.

"He is a Jew! He is a Jew!"

Another woman shouted, "Jude! Jude!" The German woman grabbed my milk container, threw my bucket to the ground in front of me. I picked it up and started walking out of the building. Several women began to shout at me.

"Dirty Jew!"

"That's what he deserves, nothing," another harped.

"Let them all starve," said another. Then they started spitting at me. One almost hit me with her drivel. Once outside I ran. I ran and ran and ran. I felt indignant; the milk wasn't for me. It was for the children. I was angry, the Poles weren't any better than the Germans. I was frightened. I never went to the dairy again.

The Polish attitude towards the Jews didn't surprise me. Anti-semitism was running rampant through Poland at that time. Even the Catholic Church was preaching openly against the Jews. The Jews had a separate society. We were second class citizens and had our own Jewish schools, sports clubs and organizations.

The next day I gathered up my courage and went to another German store. I was nervous, but I stepped up and did my 'Heil Hitler' routine. The clerk did a "Heil" back. I ordered the items on my list. Then I left the store. Once outside, I heaved a sigh of relief. I never felt as self confident as I did before the dairy incident, but I continued to stock our pantry, and many others, for some time to come.

Every day I woke up and wondered if this was the day I'd get caught, if I'd get beaten. No one knew how any day would go. And my day finally came.

I was playing with a group of friends in a courtyard that had a walk through to Sheroka Ulica. All my friends were wearing their yellow patch. I was not. Suddenly, someone hollered "Germans!" We scattered to the four corners. However, I hadn't seen them and my reaction wasn't speedy enough. By the time I turned around, one of the Germans had seen me. I started to run.

"Halt," he ordered. I looked back and saw a gun in his hand. I knew better than to try hiding.

"Come here!" I stood still. I turned to face them. One was a German National with a swastika on his arm, and the other was a German police officer.

"Come here," the German policeman yelled again. I acted like I didn't understand.

The German National said, "Come here!" in Polish. Slowly, I walked toward him. The German policeman put his gun in his holster and grabbed me by the arm.

"Are you a Jew?" he asked.

"I don't understand," I replied.

"Are you Jewish?" the German National asked in Polish again.

"NO!"

The National then told the policeman that I didn't understand German, and that I said I wasn't a Jew. But that wasn't good enough for the German policeman. He slapped my face again and again and again. My head was groggy. I could barely think. Then, he tricked me; he asked my name. I gave him a phony Polish name. He asked for my address and again I lied. He slapped me several more times.

"You report to headquarters tonight," he said. "If you don't show up, we will come and get you." He slapped me one more time.

"You are a pig," he said and then he let me go.

When the Germans had left, I stood there dazed. My friends came out of their hiding places.

"Are you going to their headquarters tonight?" they asked.

"No! I am not going anywhere near there."

They asked questions; they thought I was brave. But I didn't think so. I felt degraded. Now I knew what Father felt that night they caught him. Why didn't I do anything about it? Was I a coward? Were all Jews cowards? Would they have killed me? Could I have run away? But where would I run to?

For a few days I felt nervous. Were they looking for me? If they found me, what would happen to me? They would kill me as well as my whole family. All these things kept running through my mind. No, they won't bother to look for one Jewish kid, I hoped. Nothing happened, so I forgot the incident and everything got back to normal. I still went to the German store to get groceries and play my little game. It was almost fun to be able to get away with it.

CHAPTER IV

Now the Jewish Town Board must supply Jewish men to work for the Germans every day, but nobody wanted to. They all knew how mistreated they would be by the SS men if they went to work in their barracks. The Jewish policemen had become rough; they even had a jail in the ghetto. They put out an order for any man not reporting for work to be jailed. No one paid much attention to that order, so the policemen had to round up the men themselves. They did put a few young men in jail, but they didn't mind spending a few days there. It was better than working in the German barracks.

One day the entire Jewish police force was ordered to report to the German police headquarters. They thought they were going there for training, but it turned out to be a beating. The Germans worked them over pretty good. They weren't even told why. After that, people started snickering at the policemen. They had gotten some of their own medicine they were dishing out.

Life went on. More people were brought into the ghetto from surrounding small towns. The overcrowding was really bad now. In some cases, two families were living in one room. The two synagogues were also converted into living quarters. We were getting less bread now and the soup wasn't as good as it had been and there was much less of it. I still refused to wear the yellow patches. People were getting arrested more and more every day. No one knew why or what happened to them after their arrest.

One day we heard a story that Himmler, the chief of the SS, came to visit Plock. According to the story, he liked the town so much that he promised to give it to his SS men after it was cleaned of Poles and Jews. The story must have been true, because a few weeks after he left, Polish families were evacuated. They took their possessions on carts that they pushed or pulled as they walked to their destination. Some had horses to do this job for them. Not all of the Polish people were relocated.

A rumor started that the Jews were next to be taken, causing instant panic in the ghetto. Where would they take us? Would they allow us to take our belongings, too? They would kill us all, and soon. A week went by and nothing happened. Good! Still, we slept in our clothing. We put on two sets of clothing in case they came in the middle of the night and wouldn't allow us to take any luggage.

After a week of this, the Jewish town board put out a bulletin stating they had received assurance from the German command that the Jews would be allowed to stay here, that from now on our rations would be increased, and, as if that wasn't enough, each family would receive a pound of sugar. Everyone gave a sigh of relief that night. Everything was going to be fine now and, besides that, we could go to bed without all those extra pieces of clothing. We went to bed that night feeling more content than we had in a long time.

CHAPTER V

A few hours later, Dad was shaking my shoulder.

"Wake up, Henry! Wake up! The Germans are here. Quickly, get up and get dressed. Henry, get dressed. Now! Put on everything you can."

Screams filled the courtyard. A loud voice was yelling.

"All Jews out. All Jews out!" I dressed as fast as I could, putting on two pairs of pants and two sweaters.

"Are you ready?" Father asked. I nodded my head. An SS man appeared in the doorway. He was holding a gun up to his chest. His finger was on the trigger.

"OUT! OUT!," he shouted. He pushed each of us with his elbow while cursing.

"Dogs! Jewish pigs! Get out!"

We rushed down the stairs along with the Jankowski's and other neighbors. Marcus had a knapsack on his back, the Jankowski's were carrying a suitcase. Many people were crying or screaming or both. The courtyard was filled with SS men. They grabbed all the luggage and threw it on the ground. They punched the people with their fists as they passed by. An SS man grabbed Marcus and tried to take his knapsack.

"Give me that, you Jewish pig," he said.

"No!" cried Marcus. The SS man pulled hard. Mom reached over and took the knapsack from Marcus, handing it to the SS officer.

"It's not worth your life," Mom said.

"Run, run fast," they shouted at us. We did, we ran for our lives towards the trucks that stood in the middle of the street. A soldier lined us up like cattle, pushing and shoving us around.

"Get in the trucks. Fifty to a truck! Schnell! (quick) Schnell!" he hollered. We huddled together in fear that we would be separated.

Climbing on the truck was no easy chore. One soldier kept pushing us to the back and hitting us with a thick billy club because we weren't moving fast enough. Another soldier kept hitting us just because we were there. Dad boosted me up, then Mom and finally Marcus. My family managed to escape most of the blows but others were not so lucky. Blood covered the faces and hands of many people, young and old alike. Fifty people in a truck that was designed to carry half that. We were packed tighter than sardines. In fact, we were so close together I think we held each other up.

I could see the SS pushing a pregnant woman with a broken arm out of a house. They started beating her, hitting her on the arm and belly. She screamed for mercy. None came. She fell to the ground. Still the blows rained down on her. A man helped her up, boosted her into a truck.

The trucks began to move. As crowded as we were, there was still room for bouncing, swaying as we traveled down the bumpy, dusty road from Plock. Somehow I didn't feel too bad about leaving Plock. True, it was the town I was born in, the town I had grown up in, but the Germans had spoiled it for me. I no longer cared. But I did care about where we were going. To Germany? If not, where?

The sun rose at its scheduled time. The early morning was damp and chilly. I felt clammy. Then a sign by the side of the road read Dgaldovo. It was a town close to Muava, near the German border. The truck slammed on the brakes. We all fell forward, then backward. We had arrived at our destination. I looked out the side of the truck and saw a group of buildings surrounded by a high wire fence.

"OH!" gasped Mom. "It's a concentration camp." We looked at each other. Our faces were grim. We had heard the rumors, the stories, and now we were going to experience them. Slowly, we climbed out of the truck.

But the SS men standing by the trucks wouldn't let us go slow. They moved in and, with their clubs, began the beatings. As the people ran down the narrow road towards the gate in the middle of the high wire fence, the SS men, who had lined up on each side of the street, stepped closer and began to pummel them. People ran to avoid the beatings. Our neighbor, Frau Minski, fell but people simply trampled over or around her. The SS men continued hitting her while she was on the ground. She screamed with pain. Two young men ran over, tried to pick her up and ended up half carrying her, half dragging her away. The SS men then began beating the young men on the back. I watched in horrid fascination. Hate boiled up inside me. Why? Why? My Father's words rang in my ear.

"Because you are one of God's chosen!" No. Not any God I wanted to know.

Our truck was the next to unload. A German pulled down the back gate of the truck. People started jumping off.

"Henry, stick close me. Marcus, take care of your mother," said Dad. I ran, hand in hand, with
Father towards the building. I didn't get hit once but he did. Marcus and Mom were just behind us. Neither one of them got hit. We stood, lined up waiting to go inside. The Germans began to search everyone.

"Get out your valuables. You will have to give them up," they dictated. Mom slipped her wedding ring off.

"They'll not get this," she whispered to Dad as she put the ring in her brassiere.

The line was long. We stood in it for over an hour. I was so tired I could hardly stand up. Finally, we got to the doorway. The building was just one large room with a long table standing on the floor in the back of the room. Behind the table sat three SS men. Three boxes sat on the table. Everyone was to put their money in one box, watches and jewelry in the second box and gold and diamonds in the third. The boxes were more that half full. I had never seen so much wealth in one place in my entire life.

"Don't try to deceive us. If we find any valuables you have kept from us, you will be shot," the SS men instructed everyone. We followed the line of people to the outside of the building. An SS man stood there pointing the way with a club. I think he was tired of beating people, for he showed no inclination to hurt us in any way. However, he did shove us in the direction of a big square between the building we had just left and two long barracks. We followed the Minskis to one of them.

The 'so-called' barracks was actually an old horse stable. Straw had been thinly spread on the floor, but the smell of horse manure was still very strong. We were so tired we didn't care. We lay down and fell asleep. After a while, Marcus woke me up.

"Come with me," he said. We saw a long line outside. People were standing there, holding their containers as one SS man ladled out soup and the other one beat the person as he passed.

"Hungry?" asked Marcus.

"Yes, very hungry. And I don't even care if I get hit with the club."

"Okay, just run fast when you get the soup." When my turn came, I kept one eye on the soup and the other on the club. Just as I approached the man dishing out the soup, the man with the club turned and looked the other way. Something had attracted his attention. Luckily we escaped yet another blow. We took the soup to share with Mom and Dad. We had no spoons, so we drank it. It was like water but it provided some nourishment for our hollow bellies.

There were no lights at night. We sat in the dark. Some people whispered. Everyone wondered what would happen to us. We were afraid to speak aloud, afraid that talking would carry the death penalty.

A little later, I had to go to the bathroom. I couldn't see a thing. I tried to pick my way through the sleeping bodies on the floor. I stumbled over many, but no one complained. Everyone had sympathy for me because they knew that sooner or later they would experience the same. Once outside, under the camp lights, I found a hole near one side of the building. This was our bathroom.

The next morning I awoke to screams. A pregnant woman had gone into labor. Another woman shouted for blankets. Someone who had been prepared for the evacuation had packed some belongings. Two were found. Several women volunteered to act as midwives and a few others held up the blanket so the poor woman could have some privacy. This was my first inkling of what childbirth was about. I was frightened; her screams sent chills through my body.

An SS man walked in.

"What are all the screams about?" he demanded. Then he

noticed the women holding up the blankets. He walked over and looked around the side. Astonished, he shouted,

"Sing! Everybody sing. This is a happy occasion. A baby is being born." Everyone was shocked. Someone started to sing 'Hatikva,' an old Jewish hymn.

Soon the barracks were filled with the sounds of music. We sang as loud as we could. I wondered about this world and the Germans. In one instance, we were afraid to talk in normal voices for fear of being killed; in the next, we were singing at the top of our lungs. And why were we singing? The baby? To be born into this? What kind of a future was there for that innocent child? But the singing was good. It cheered our hearts. The SS man seemed to enjoy it, too. I wonder if he would have liked the song so much if he had known that, instead of the regular phrases, the Jews were hurling curse words against him and his compatriots. Finally, there was a squeak, then a cry. It was a boy. Mazeltov! Congratulations and good luck! A new life had been brought into the world. The SS man returned.

"Is the baby born yet?" he asked.

"Yes. It is a boy." His face lit up with smiles. He walked to the baby, picked it up and held it gently in his arms.

"Does the baby have a name?"

"No," the mother answered.

"Good! Then I will give him a name. His name will be Joseph Von Dgaldov." The he returned the baby to the mother. When he left, the people began to sing again. He seemed pleased. Half an hour later he returned with a loaf of bread and a bottle of milk and gave them to the mother.

"This bread is for you. You will need to get strong to care for the baby. The milk is for the baby. Rest! Take care of him," he said.

Meanwhile, we were hungry and had nothing to do as the day dragged by. None of us had eaten since yesterday. I wanted something to eat, even the watered down soup would taste good. But I was afraid of the beating that would come with it.

An SS man came in.

"I need four volunteers to come with me," he said. "You will work in the kitchen." Four of the men did go with him. I stood by the door watching, wondering if they would return. Soon they came back carrying two big containers of soup. Two SS men served the soup. Obviously, it was going to be the same: a bowl of soup and a blow to the body, maybe two or three if you didn't move fast enough. I sat down by Mom and Dad.

"My back is hurt," complained Dad. I think they hit me in the ribs."

"I will go get the soup," I said.

"No, no," Mom said. "Don't worry about me so. I can do it. Then go, I will stay with your father. But be careful."

The line wasn't as long as it had been yesterday. I wondered if some people would rather go hungry than get beaten. I stood in the line watching what would continue to be a familiar scene. First the soup was served, then the club came down – on the head- on the back- in the ribs- somewhere the club came down and landed hard. Suddenly, I noticed that today's SS man with the club was the same man that had given the new baby a name. He had brought milk and bread for the mother. Maybe this one had some kind of heart somewhere under that loathsome uniform. My heart began to pound loud and furiously. One SS man poured the soup into my container. I watched, waited for the club to come down on me. I hesitated for a moment looking at him and in return he looked at me.

"Well! What are you waiting for? Do you want to get hit? Get out of here," he shouted.

I started running. Maybe this man liked kids. I ran back to the barracks. I told Mom, Dad and Marcus what had happened, but I could tell they didn't believe me. Mom looked at me affectionately and patted me on the back. I quickly grabbed the other container.

"I'll get more soup," I shouted as I ran out. There was no line. What would I do? I just shrugged my shoulders and walked over to the SS men.

"Could I have some more soup?" I asked. They were surprised. They looked at me dumbfounded for a second, then they poured more soup into my container. I turned and walked back to the barracks. Twice! Twice I had avoided getting hit.

But that was not all for the soup line that day. One of the SS men came in waving his club around.

"Go, get some soup. Don't you want to eat? You Jewish pigs. Maybe you think our soup is not good enough for you. Get up. Get out there," he shouted while chasing people out the door.

Not much happened the next day. But the following day (the fourth day) a train came in to camp. SS men were all over. Did this mean we were leaving? Where would we go next? Would it be better? It couldn't be worse. One of the SS men pulled out a list. He began to bellow out names. People filed outside as their names were called. Then our name was called. I didn't want to go, but I didn't want to be shot either. I did as I was told. They lined up us by the open boxcars. Two SS men were handing out rations of bread. Mom, Dad, Marcus and I received half a loaf of bread. I wondered how long the bread would have to last. Then the SS men began to shove and push us around.

"Hurry up. Everyone, hurry up!" they shouted. We climbed into a box car while the SS men counted heads. Sixty to a car. It was crowded. But some were able to sit down. Since there was not enough room for everyone to sit at the same time, it was decided that we would take turns. There was no straw on the floor to soften the hard surface. We waited on the tracks for an hour before the train started moving. Which way were we going?

CHAPTER VI

The train climbed the hill slowly and went down faster on the other side. We had been riding all day; night was setting in. Soon we would not be able to see the countryside we were traveling through. Some suggested that we were headed for Warsaw. Were they right? The villages got closer and closer together. It was more than likely that we were approaching a big town. The lights of the city came into view and the train slowed to a stop. We discovered that we were in Praga, a suburb of Warsaw. After a wait of fifteen minutes, the train began to move again. Instead of going to Warsaw, the train made its way into the country and away from the city. I fell asleep.

When I woke it was to the sway of the boxcar, the clackety clack of the train wheels.

"Where are we?" I asked. No one knew.

"Here, Henry, have some bread" said Father.

"Is this all there is?"

"Yes, we saved the last piece for you." I looked at the small bit of crust. Then I ate it, slowly so the flavor would last. I couldn't think of anything but food. I was so hungry. No matter how I tried to dwell on other things, I couldn't stop thinking about food.

Late the following day, the train pulled into Chmielnik. When we left the train, the Germans lined us up and marched us into town. We saw a few Polish policemen and many Jewish policemen. The Jewish policemen wore hats and armbands of white with the star of David in the middle. They also carried billy clubs. It felt good to be walking, to stretch our legs after so much time in the boxcar. Originally, Chmielnik had a population of three thousand. Now, so many Jews had been shipped in from all over Poland, that its population had grown to ten thousand. Most of the Christians lived on the outskirts of town while Jews occupied the town itself. Chmielnik was so crowded that two and three families were living in one room. Nonetheless, we were pleased to be there among our fellow man.

A Jewish policeman came and took us to a big synagogue. "Someone from the local area will come take your family to a house," he told us. While we were sitting on a bench waiting, they distributed food and water. Nothing ever tasted better.

A woman came over and asked, "How many are in your family?"

"Four," said Father. "My wife and these two boys."

"I have a room at the back of my store. You could stay there for a while." We were happy. Our joy was short-lived; we spent the night sleeping sitting up on the one lonely cot. At least we felt safe.

When we woke the next morning, the lady told us we had to go register with the Jewish town board. Arriving at the town board, we found many people from Plock. Some were still staying at the synagogue. There was nowhere else for them to go, and no one had money for anything. Everything valuable had been turned over to the Germans.

The Jewish officials were very sympathetic, but they were helpless. Too many people; too little resources. We were given ration cards that entitled us to receive a slab of bread and a bowl of soup each day. The bread tasted awful. It was a black bread made with very little flour, lots of potatoes and wheat chaff. But, for those of us who were hungry, it tasted just fine. The soup had very little meat, but remembering that beggars couldn't be choosers, we ate. Again, the soup was stirred in such a way that the vegetables and meats stayed in the bottom of the pot. Those ingredients were either sold on the black market or saved for the kitchen help to eat. All food was prepared and distributed in the communal kitchen.

Returning to our quarters we were met by the landlady. "I am sorry," she said. "The room I have given you is too small for your family. I talked it over with my neighbors and they agreed to take each one of you in. Even though you will be separated, it will be better than all four of you sleeping on that one small cot."

I went to a family that had three children, all much older than me. I had to sleep with the youngest son who was ten years older than me. They were nice people. The next day they invited me for supper. Supper was very good. It was the first time I sat at a table for quite some time. I felt like a human, at last.

The next morning, Dad, Mom, Marcus and I got together. Although each one of us had been treated very well, we didn't want to overstay our welcome.

"Let's see if we can't find our own place to stay," suggested Marcus.

"I'll go talk to some of the barbers here in town," said Dad. "Maybe one of them will go into business with me. We could support ourselves. I have a few tools the Germans didn't get." But there weren't many places to stay, especially without money. We had no choice but to depend on the goodness of others.

For several weeks we were in limbo. Then good fortune smiled on us. Father and another barber got together and found a vacant store they could use for a barbershop. Shortly after that, we were able to find a room. The only piece of furniture in the room was a wooden bunk. When it was filled with straw, it would do very nicely. Unfortunately, the barbershop did very little business. The only people who came to him were his old customers from Plock and most of them had no money. Father often cut hair for nothing but the privilege of keeping busy.

The food situation got worse. Most of the time we went hungry.

Winter set in, but the room had no stove to warm us. We weren't the only ones hungry and freezing. Our people, the Jews, were dying slowly, one by one. Father's health had not been good since he was hit in the back at Dgaldovo.

The winter passed. Spring was more than welcome. The weather warmed up and all of a sudden things looked as though they might get better. Many of the boys and girls were going to work in the surrounding villages as farm hands. I wanted to go. It would help my family. They would have more food, I would, too.

"I don't want you to go," said Mom. "You're just a baby."

"Just a baby? Mom, I'm twelve years old. Besides, after this last year I think I've grown up a lot."

Sighing, she spoke, "I suppose."

"It will be good for all of us," said Father. "Henry will be a good worker."

Mom gave in and the next morning I set out to find a job. Keep in mind that at this time farmers in Poland lived under very primitive conditions. Most of them lived in one-room huts with straw roofs. I approached the first farmer I met.

"Have you any jobs I might do for you?" I asked. "I am young and strong and willing to do almost any kind of work."

"No. I don't need any help. But my neighbor needs someone to tend to his cows. He lives down the road."

With barely a word, he hired me. I became a working man. His family was small. He had a wife and a small baby girl. They were a very nice family.

"Come in, sit down and have some lunch," they said. They served soup and bread. I sat at the table and ate all my stomach would hold. It was the first time in well over a year. Then I thought about Father, Mom and Marcus. I felt guilty for having eaten so much when they were still hungry.

After lunch, the farmer showed me around his farm. He grew tobacco, potatoes and corn. His livestock consisted of two cows and a horse. It was the habit of Polish farmers to cultivate all of their land save for a strip on which the livestock were to graze. His was a long narrow strip about twenty feet wide and perhaps a quarter of a mile long. Potatoes were planted on one side and corn on the other. My job would be to keep the livestock on this thin strip of land.

Returning from the fields, he showed me his barn. It was a large wooden building with a loft and a few stalls for the animals. The rest of the barn was being used to hang and store the tobacco. I had never seen tobacco hanging before. There were rows and rows of tobacco leaves drying. The odor was overwhelming.

"Here, you can sleep up here," he told me. That scared me. I thought I would be able to sleep in the house. I had never slept anywhere alone before.

Supper was a pleasant time. They asked about my family and seemed quite sympathetic about our situation.

After supper, the farmer said, "When the sun goes down, it is time for bed." With that, he lit a lantern and led the way out to the barn. "Here you are. Have a good night's sleep. I will wake you up at the crack of dawn." He held the light for me as I made my way up the ladder to the loft. Then he left.

It was now pitch black. I took off my jacket and lay down on the hay. I tried to cover myself with the hay, but I always moved and knocked it off, thereby getting a drafty spot. It was comfortable enough, but I was scared. I imagined mice and rats running all over me. I was afraid of them. Every little noise startled me. Finally, I fell asleep.

"Henry. Henry. Wake up. It's time for work." I made my way down the ladder, happy to leave the loft. "Here, here is a bucket of water for you to wash up with. Wash and then come to breakfast." There was no soap or towel, so I wiped myself off with the end of my shirt. Then I went to breakfast.

There was a big plate of steaming food on the table. It was some sort of mush and I didn't think it tasted too good. I ate it anyway. When we finished, the farmer led me to the barn. He unlocked the stalls that held the two cows. Each one came out wearing a rope around its neck. They walked right out of the barn and stood there. Just like they were waiting for me.

"Here, don't be afraid," said the farmer. "Cows are gentle creatures. They won't hurt you. Remember the grazing place. Take the cows there and see that they don't get into the corn or the potatoes. At high noon, they will lead you home."

I took the ends of the ropes and the cows started walking out of the yard. Sure enough, they led me right to the grazing spot. I tried to keep them in the middle but they always seemed to make their way to the sides. I had thought this job was going to be easy, but by noon I was worn out from chasing them. Then the cows started walking home. I wondered how they could tell time. When they got to the barn, they walked right into their own stalls. I chained them up and gave them some hay.

Lunch was ready and waiting for me, boiled potatoes and a watery, sour soup. It tasted good. They also served big chunks of dark bread. It was SO good. My stomach was full again.

After lunch, I went and got the cows to go back to the field again. It was the same thing as in the morning. I chased those cows from one side to the other. First away from the corn, and then away from the potatoes. When the sun started to set on the horizon, the cows headed for the barn on their own. Again I put them in their stalls, locked them up with the chain and went to wash up.

Supper! Worn out from chasing the cows, I ate well and then went to the loft for sleep. I knew I would never get used to this kind of life. There was not much to talk about with the farmer and his wife, and there sure wasn't anybody else. And I hated being alone as much as I hated sleeping in the loft. I had tried for five days and just couldn't take it. The work wasn't hard. I was getting used to the cows, but I was too lonely. I talked with the farmer.

"I understand," he said. With those words we parted and I went back to my family.

Walking towards Chmielnik I wondered if I had done the right thing. I wasn't helping by returning; in fact, it was the opposite. I would be another mouth to feed and with rations so sparse, well, I wouldn't be an asset. Maybe I could find a job in town.

Soon I entered Chmielnik. There were red tags on many of the buildings. People walked quickly by those places. I stopped to read one of the tags. In black letters the sign read TYPHOID FEVER and underneath KEEP OUT. What was typhoid fever? I had never heard of it. Was the house we lived in tagged? Would I be able to see my family? I rushed home. Thank God, there was no tag on our apartment house.

Mother greeted me at the door with open arms. "I am so glad you are home. We missed you so much. How are you? What brings you home? Are you well?"

"I am fine, Mom but how are you?"

"I am worried about your Father. He is not well. He has been in bed for three days now. He has a lot of pain in his back."

"Did you call a Doctor?"

Mom looked thinner, more stooped and a great deal more tired. "Of course, but the doctors are so busy with the typhoid epidemic they can't get around to everyone. Here, come see your Father." Father smiled a hello and reached for my hand.

"I am so glad to see you son." It was easy to see that talking gave him immense pain. I sat down by his bed.

"Mother, what's typhoid fever?" I asked.

"It's a very high fever. It is very contagious and almost certain death."

"Father?"

"No, he has no fever, just the pain," said Mother. "Maybe when the SS man hit him?" Father turned his eyes to the ceiling.

"Where does typhoid fever come from?" I asked.

"From dirt, sometimes from lice. The way we are forced to live, its no wonder we have it. Many families that we knew from home are dying. Oh, its terrible to see the toll typhoid takes."

"Where's Marcus," I asked.

"He has a job tutoring a young Polish Christian girl. Sometimes they feed him. He gets paid a few Zlotys each week. It helps. Once in a while, they even send some food home for us, your Father and me."

I stayed home for two weeks and with each day that passed I grew hungrier. Father lay in bed; pain raged through his body. At night, we could hear him moan and groan in a fitful sleep. Sometimes Father seemed like his old self and other times he didn't know who we were.

Finally, the doctor came to see him. "It is his lungs. There is nothing that can be done for him except to make him as comfortable as you can," he said.

"No!" I said to myself. "He will not die." I could not, would not accept his death.

Several days later I met a friend from back home on the street. I was amazed. We used to be friends in Plock, and I hadn't seen him since.

"Henry, I can't believe my eyes. How are you? What are you doing here?"

"The same thing everyone else is," I answered. "I'm looking for work."

"I just came from a distant village. Its about twenty kilometers from here. It's nice there. The people are very friendly. The farmer I work for gave me twenty-five pounds of potatoes and a couple loaves of bread to bring home to my family. I have just come to deliver them and stay for a short visit."

"Are there more good jobs up there?"

"Sure! In fact, the farmer I work for is looking for a boy to tend his cows."

"He is? Where do I find him?" He gave me directions. I had to do some pretty fast talking for her to let me go.

"Father is too sick," I said. "You need the rations for yourself and him, and I'm not doing any good here. Besides, I can take care of myself."

The next morning I said a special goodbye to Father. Mom walked out of the room with me. We both had tears in our eyes.

"Pray for your Father," she said as I walked down the stairs.

CHAPTER VII

I looked over my shoulders every now and then as I walked down the highway to the city. I watched for any Germans that might be in the area. I didn't want to be caught. It was against the law for Jews to leave town, punishable by death, of course! I let the main highway and took a country road. It was a long walk to get there, but I had no troubles of any kind.

This village was bigger than the one I had worked in before. I found the farmer I was supposed to see with minimum trouble. His house was the biggest, nicest house in the village. He had two sons and a daughter. His livestock consisted of eight cows and two horses.

I introduced myself and asked, "Do you need help with the work here?" We talked for a bit and then he said,

"Yes, I need the help. Can you start right away?"

His house was very large, but it was only one room with two beds and a big bench by the stove.

"This is where you will sleep," he told me, pointing to the bench. My face lit up in smiles. I wouldn't be alone and I wouldn't be in a loft where mice or rats could get to me.

The farmer's barn was apart from his house. And he had another separate building for his eight cows. He was very well-to-do. Later, I found out he was the village chairman. I fretted, remembering how I had chased two cows from one side to the other; how would I handle eight cows?

His children were older than me. The oldest boy was twenty-five, the girl was twenty and the youngest boy was eighteen. Anna did the housework, since her mother had died two years earlier. Anna was a good cook and the food was very good. Much better than the last farmer's place!

The next morning, after a good night's sleep and a good breakfast, the farmer told me, "Follow the cows. You will meet up with some other boys. Walk with them to the grazing place."

I did as instructed and in no time at all I met up with two other boys about the same age as I. We talked as we followed the cows. It was a long walk and by the time we got to the grazing pasture we had become good friends. This village had several grazing areas and we took turns going from one to the other. There were several marshes around the village so watching the cows was not as demanding as I thought it would be. It was more fun, too. We baked potatoes over an open fire, and we caught fish and cooked them in the same manner. Time went by fast and I looked forward to work each day.

Then one night, after three weeks had passed, I didn't sleep well. I woke up covered with a cold sweat. I had the strangest feeling. Something was not right with Dad. I couldn't sleep the rest of the night.

A week after that restless night, my friends and I were walking the cows back home. As we approached the village, I saw a man's figure standing alone. Somehow that man's way of standing was familiar to me. Then I recognized him. It was Marcus. I ran to him.

"Is it Dad?" I asked. I could not stop the tears from rolling down my face, nor did I try. Marcus opened his arms to me. I fell into them and we stood there, both of us crying. Once I stopped shaking, Marcus held me at arm's length.

"Are you okay," asked Marcus.

"Yes. Tell me about Dad."

"He died about a week ago in his sleep."

"Why didn't you come get me. I would have liked to go the funeral."

"You couldn't come. They buried him the very next day. With all the typhoid in the town, they aren't taking any extra chances. Besides, you are so far away you wouldn't have made it back in time anyhow."

"How is Mother?"

"She is doing very well. But I am worried about her. She is very depressed and losing weight. I want to talk to your boss and explain how thinks are, what has happened."

Marcus went to the farmer, who offered to help, "Here, take some potatoes back to your mother. Tell her to eat. She will get stronger if she eats well."

Then it was time for Marcus to leave if he was to get home before the curfew.

"Be careful going back to Chmielnik. Ge before it gets dark," I said. "And take good care of Mother."

"Don't worry. I will."

We shook hands goodbye and embraced each other one last time. I watched him walk down the road thinking how tall he was for a boy seventeen years old. I wondered if I would ever see him again. When he disappeared from view, I went back to the farm.

"I'm sorry. Very sorry. Come in," said the farmer.

I entered the house and sat down on the bench. The family sat down at the table to eat.

"Come, join us," he said.

"I'm not hungry," I answered. Nor could I sleep. Why? Why? Why? I wondered. Eventually, I fell asleep.

I was moody and depressed the next few days. I felt alone, that I was the only one in the world who had experienced a loss. The hate that I thought I had set aside returned twofold. It was the Germans, the damn Germans. They were the ones who were treating the Jews like animals, like ragdolls thrown aside, as if we didn't matter at all.

Summer was coming to an end. We had just harvested the wheat. The sharp ends of the straw cut into my bare feet. We heard that Germans had come into a neighboring village, caught a Jewish boy working for one of the local farmers. They shot him on site. Three of us worked handling cows in this village.

"We'd better leave," I said.

"Right! We'd be killed," agreed my friend.

The farmer wasn't very happy. "You've been a good worker. I hate to see you go."

"My being here would only endanger you and your family," I said.

"Yes, you are right about that. Give me your address. I will bring you a sack of potatoes." With that promise I set off for

Chmielnik.

Things hadn't changed much. Rations were still very skimpy. The typhoid fever was still raging through town and people looked sick as ever. Mom was happy to see me.

"Mom, you don't look good. Are you all right? Are you getting enough to eat?"

"I'm all right. Don't worry about me. But I am worried about Marcus," she answered, coughing.

"Why? Where is he?"

The Germans have taken him, along with two hundred other young men. He is at a work camp about ten miles from here. They say the first two hundred will be replaced after two months. Then Marcus should be home, but I am afraid."

A month passed. Mother and I had no money for food or anything else. We lived on a small portion of soup and a piece of bread allotted to us by our ration cards. I hung around the railway yard waiting for trains to come in. Each time a train pulled into the station, I looked for Marcus and food.

Sometimes the boxcars had potatoes, sometimes coal. I and other kids tried to steal whatever we could. Working in pairs we accomplished quite a bit this way. One snuck up on top of the cars and threw down potatoes or coal whichever they had. Later, we divided up the loot. It was dangerous. The train was guarded by the Polish police who carried guns. They would have used then on us if we had been caught.

A new order was issued: All Jews between the ages of twelve and forty must report to the Market Square for registration within two days. The Germans were going to take the young people to work. There was nothing new in that statement; they were doing that already! Nothing to worry about. After all, they didn't say anything about bringing belongings, so they were not taking anyone anywhere.

The next morning I went down to the Market Square bright and early. There were lots of people milling around. At each corner were Jewish and Polish policemen. They let people into the square, but they wouldn't let anyone out. People got nervous. They couldn't understand why there were no German soldiers around. What was going on? No one would answer our questions. Suddenly, there was a big commotion. A staff car with three German officers pulled up in the square followed by a truck full of German soldiers. The soldiers jumped off the truck and took positions at the perimeter of the square. Then empty trucks drove in, forming a line. Soldiers started to shove us.

"Line up," they shouted.

The German soldiers started walking down the lines. Older men and women and children were pushed to one side, young men and women to the other. All the young people were loaded on the trucks. When it came to my turn, a soldier pushed me toward some older people and children who were standing near. As he pushed me, I bumped into a German officer. For a moment I thought I would get a beating because it was against the law for a Jew to touch a German uniform. To my surprise, he grabbed me and pushed me the other way. Before I realized what had happened, I found myself on one of the trucks.

I pushed my way to the side of the truck, figuring that when the truck would be moving, I wouldn't fall. I stood on the truck watching. The selection was almost over. A dozen trucks had been loaded with people. Big crowds of people stood at each corner of the square, watching, wondering, where the trucks were going, trying to get to the trucks to say goodbye to their loved ones. The Jewish and Polish police held them back. When the last of the trucks were loaded, the police let the crowd go. People ran from one truck to the next, searching for the loved ones. With tears running down their faces, they looked in each truck.

One woman cried out for someone. A little girl looked for her brother. She was running along the line of trucks, looking for her brother, calling his name. In her arms she was clutching a whole loaf of bread. Crying, she ran down the line. As she came to the truck I was on, a Jewish policeman suddenly appeared next to her and grabbed the loaf of bread from her hand and threw it toward the truck where I was standing. I caught the bread. All of a sudden, I felt rich, I would be eating good today. It had been a long time since I had eaten so much bread. It was like a piece of gold to me.

The little girl was becoming hysterical and begged me to give the bread back to her. Now I started to fight with myself. The policeman gave me the bread –it's mine! And then I looked in her eyes and it was like she touched my soul and I threw the bread back to her.

The hysterics of the crowd continued to a higher level, but the trucks began to move. I looked for Mom, but I couldn't see her anywhere. As the trucks moved out of the square and down Main Street, they picked up speed.

"Wait!" I screamed. "There she is. My Mother." She stood there on the sidewalk crying. She looked at each truck as it went by.

"Mother! Mother!" I yelled. She didn't notice me. "Oh stop, please stop so I can say goodbye to her. So I can hug her, give her a kiss. Why can't you do that? You have taken everything away from her. Her home, her furniture, her security, her husband and now you are taking me, her last son. Please stop."

CHAPTER VIII

The trucks rolled down the highway. My tears had dried up and I concentrated on maintaining my balance. I was lucky, for I could hold on to the side. The driver seemed to delight in slowing and revving up the engine. It made for a very jerky ride. The people in the middle had a hard time of it.

People talked and speculated as to what would happen to them. I didn't participate in their guessing games; I had played those silly pastimes before and nothing we had thought came in to being anyhow. Just take what comes, I said to myself.

Hours passed. Some of the men knew the area and, every time we passed a village, they started another guessing contest.

"We're going towards the Russian border," said one. "No, no! We are going towards--? I was bored with it all. After four hours had passed, we came to Skarzysko-Kamenia.

"This is where the big ammunition factories are," a man told me.

The trucks turned to the left and drove down a dirt road through a forest. The road led to a clearing and we saw a big factory surrounded by a barbed wire fence. The trucks stopped at a large gate guarded by a sentry. The gates parted and the trucks drove through. Then the Germans opened the back end of the trucks screaming,

"Get out. Move it. Line up over here." We saw Jewish policemen. There must be other Jews here, I thought.

Once unloaded, the truck evacuated the area. We stood for a long time. It was another war of nerves. Finally, a German officer in a green field uniform came out of a building. He started screaming at us.

"It is an honor to work for the war machinery of the Third Reich. We have three factories in this complex, A, B and C. You are in camp A now, but you will be separated and assigned to work in one of the three factories. The selection will begin immediately." We didn't know whether to applaud or shout Heil Hitler.

Jewish policemen had taken positions along each side of the building. The selection began. Two girls sat inside the building behind a big desk. One was typing, the other was asking questions. Name, age, sex and so on. I was assigned to factory B.

I went back outside. There was still a long line to register. I was very hungry but there was no food. The Jewish policeman shifted us into three groups. Approximately one hundred men and women were in my group. We were escorted to our concentration camp within the boundaries of factory B.

It was late fall and the temperature was dropping. I was cold, so very cold and hungry. Very, very hungry. A guard walked over to our group. He was wearing a different color uniform, light brown. I learned that these guards were camp guards, the Ukrainians. They were the men who hated Russia so much that they volunteered to join the German army. I didn't think the Germans trusted them enough to let them fight in the front lines, so they made them concentration camp guards. And they were mean. They hated the Russians, but they hated the Jews more. They would kill instantly, for no reason.

We marched five miles from the factory to camp B in the forest. The guard marched so fast some of us had to run to keep up with him. By the time we arrived in camp, I was no longer cold. On the contrary, I was sweating. When we got to the gate, I didn't care about anything. I wanted to lay down right there and go to sleep. But they opened the gate for us and marched us to the barracks. The camp wasn't very big. There were only eight buildings surrounding a very small yard. When the guard left, the Jewish policemen took over.

"You will all sleep in this barracks," we were told.

There were no cots, no straw. I didn't care. I was too tired, but the policeman kept us lined up. He counted and recounted until he was satisfied that no one had escaped.

"There is no food for you. You have arrived too late. Tomorrow at noon you will receive your rations. You will also be assigned your work station tomorrow." With those words he left us.

I found comfort in meeting a boy who was the same age as I. We lay down on the floor together.

"My family came from Lodz originally," he said. "We spent some time in Chmielnik before we came here.

"My family came from Plock. We have been several places; the last one was Cmielnik, too." He spoke Polish as I did. "I think we should learn Yiddish because all the other Jews speak Yiddish," I said. "We might save ourselves some trouble if we can get along better."

"I think you're right," he replied. It took us several weeks before we understood Yiddish reasonably well. Once we learned, we got along better with the other Jews. We were also able to communicate words and ideas we didn't want the Poles to hear.

That night I fell into a deep sleep. Someone was calling my name. "Henry, Henry, wake up!" I opened by eyes to see a young man standing over me.

"Do you remember me? Your brother's friend! I am one of the first ones to come here when they first built the camp. I've been here for almost eight months now." I looked him up and down. He was dressed nice, wearing English riding boots, English breeches and a nice fitted jacket.

"Are you some kind of big shot? I asked him.

"I am a foreman in the factory. Have you had anything to eat today?"

"No, not since the day before."

"I will get you something." He returned with a piece of bread and a container of cold soup. "Keep the container and spoon. You will need it. Don't leave it anywhere, someone will steal it. Now, don't worry, I will take case of you." He stood up smiling. "Good night. I will see you tomorrow." I lay back down feeling comforted. I knew someone here, and he was a big shot. He would look after me.

My friend woke up. He was jealous of me for I had the bread my brother's friend had given me. I broke it up.

"Here, for you," I offered.

"Up! Everybody up!" the Jewish policeman shouted as he walked through the barracks. "Up and be out in the yard in fifteen minutes." We left the barracks to find the washroom. Washroom!

What a laugh. There was cold water, no soap and no towels. We washed our faces and dried them on our shirts. Then we hurried to the yard.

"Newcomers, move to one side," the policeman yelled. They counted the people again. I noticed others had been standing outside longer than us. They were the old ones, the ones who had been here for a long time, six months to a year. Their faces were pale, almost ghostly and they looked half starved. They wore rags and their heads were shaved. They looked like scarecrows Every person carried a container for food. I wondered how long it would be before I looked like that. No, never, I vowed.

When the counting was done, the crowd was divided into two groups. Each foreman took one group and marched them out of the gate.

"Newcomers, line up!" the policeman shouted.

We stood in line for a long time. Nothing happened. Some men came through the gate accompanied by a woman. They looked different, nicely dressed and well fed. These were the German bosses. They walked over to our line and started to make selections. I was chosen by Pavloski and his wife Bertha. Pavlowski, Bertha and a man named Krause, ran the department in the factory that made blank rifle bullets which were used for practice. After the selections had been made, we reported to the barber for a haircut. Two barbers worked rapidly as they cut our hair. There were no mirrors, so we had no idea of what we looked like. My friend and I met outside. We looked at each other and laughed. We both looked funny.

Noon time arrived. Two policemen carried in large soup containers. One dished the soup out, the other stirred, but only the top of the soup. The heavy pieces, the good pieces of meat or whatever vegetables there were, sank to the bottom. None of us got them. When they finished serving our rations, they kept the rest to sell or to eat themselves.

"Do you know what kind of soup this?" I asked my friend. "I'm not sure. Maybe kohlrabi?" The soup was filling when eaten, but it didn't last long. Soon, you were as hungry as before.

"Tomorrow, tomorrow you will go to work," the policeman informed us.

My friend and I had been chosen to work in separate places. But that didn't mean we couldn't stay in the same barracks. The first one we visited smelled so strongly of body odor we almost gagged. The barracks was half empty. Some people were sleeping in the bunks which had two tiers Some were sitting around talking to each other. A few even spent their energy arguing.

A young man, maybe two years older than I told us, "I've been here for four months. We all work twelve hour shifts. Every Sunday, the shift changes. You work one week of days and one week of nights."

"Why is the barracks half full?" my friend asked.

"They made room for you newcomers. Just about every two weeks, the German bosses make new selections. The weak men, the sick men go to camp C in the forest and are shot. Then a new shipment of Jews, like you, come to replace them. Another thing, don't think any bunk is yours. You share it with whoever is working the opposite shift of you. I have good advice for you. Don't get sick. Stay healthy."

"How," I asked, "on one ladle of that soup they serve? That small slice of bread?"

"Listen, two days in a row, just two days in the barracks and you're a dead man."

We soon found out that one of the worst persons to deal with was Jarmolof. He was a weasel of a man even though he was Jewish. Originally, he came from the town of Radom. He was short, thin and carried a rubber hose split on the ends, much like a cat o'nine tails whip. He used it on anybody, anytime he felt like it. They told us he used to be a religious Hasidic scholar. What could have happened to him to make him such a monster? His assistant, Sigmund, also came from the same town. He was heavy, short and stocky with a mustache that looked like it has been painted on under his nose. Re resembled a butcher and he, too, carried a long piece of rubber hose with split ends. If you got in his way, you suffered for it. They swung those hoses wildly, hitting any part of your body they could reach, head, shoulders, back. When their arms tired of wielding the rubber hose, they kicked men in the groin and women in the backside.

The day shift came back to the barracks and my friend and I were able to find a place to sleep. There were no mattresses, only straw. No one undressed. But I took off my jacket to cover myself. At that point I still had decent clothes to wear.

Once a month, on Sundays, we were allowed a shower at camp A. This was a good thing, for the camps were infested with lice. As we showered, our clothes were steamed. Hopefully that would kill the small creatures. But it was only a temporary stop gap. Besides, after your clothes were steamed a few times, they were reduced to rags.

I was nervous as I went to my first day of work.

"You are lucky to be picked for this department," an old man told me. "The work is not too hard. It's reasonably clean and the bosses aren't too bad."

I looked at the building ahead of me. It was a big building with three stories and big steel windows. It was divided into three rooms with an office on one side. In the middle were two big machines. At one end of the machine, a worker fed the empty rifle shells. Powder was poured from the top into the shells. Then they were fed to the next machine which had a flat bed where the steel plates were fed. The plates had holes on the flat part. These holes were filled with felt. The felt was pressed into the bullets, and a wooden tip came down on each bullet which made it a finished product. It was all mechanized. It only took two people to operate those machines.

On the other side of the room was a small machine that pushed felt into the steel plates. This was to be my job. A female Jewish boss showed me how to do it. It was easy. I fed steel plates in one end, inserted squares of felt on top and removed the plates from the other side. Then I stacked the plates on the opposite side of the machine.

The boss warned me, "Be sure you have plenty of full plates ahead. That way you won't slow down production for the war effort."

At first I worked hard, quickly worrying that I wouldn't have enough plates. I was afraid they would yell and scream at me. But, I soon figured out that my machine was faster than the big one. I always had enough plates handy to be at least one hour ahead of the big machine.

The third, and last, room had six small machines where they pressed on the bottom of the bullets. Then the bullets were packed and transported to the first room. There were many small tables in that room. Girls sat at those tables using small instruments to inspect each bullet for its precision. Then the bullets went to another table where girls packed them in small boxes. A dozen in each box, then into a larger box. On the outside of each box was a woven cloth belt fastened on the top. Men loaded the cartons onto hand carts and then the boxes were transported to the warehouse.

My work was easy, but monotonous. I was able to go to the bathroom whenever I needed. I liked to go because there was always some man or woman that had news from other parts of the compound.

There were two other departments in the factory. One department manufactured two millimeter bullets, the other produced machine gun bullets. Laidwig was the boss of the two millimeter bullet division. The boss of the other department was Hering, a German. They both had the reputation of being the meanest, the most horrid bosses in the entire factory. On the second floor of Hering's department was the Music Room. It was a place where, whenever bosses felt like it, they took people for beatings. Either one of them would order the Jewish foreman to beat whoever they had in custody. And, of course, the Jewish foreman did so for, if he didn't, he was beaten or shot. Men and women alike were selected for this form of torture while the bosses watched. Sometimes, all the bosses watched. Pavlowski's wife, Bertha, was always there.

I was hungry all the time. I recalled that I had turned my nose up at some of the foods Mom served. I wouldn't do that again. Food took up the major portion of my thoughts. I counted the hours until they brought the soup. I held my container very carefully so I wouldn't spill a drop. I treated my soup like it was a treasured liquid. It was a precious liquid, as precious as the blood flowing through my veins. I sat and ate slowly to prolong the enjoyment as long as I could. My container didn't have to be washed. I licked it clean every day. Many fought over a second serving of soup like animals. I guarded my soup zealously for I knew it was my survival.

The policemen and Bertha often watched while people struggled to get a second helping. Always, those who tried were beaten. The amazing thing about that was some people no longer cared how hard the blows fell on their backs. I don't think they even felt it. They were just intent on more soup. Two short weeks provided me with this education. How long would I last before I would be reduced to that state?

But, I was often able to leave my machine at work and go to the kitchen before noon. I found many good things to eat behind the garbage can. Pieces of potatoes, a bone with some meat on or some vegetables. Even a bone was a find; I could suck the juices out.

Bread was supposed to be distributed evenly, but the camp commandant got just so many loaves. He cut smaller portions off for the workers and saved bigger quantities for the foreman and the policeman. The bread wasn't that good anyway, except if you were starving to death. It was black, supposedly rye, but I think there were more potatoes in it than anything else, including flour. It was heavy and so slimy that it could have been used to plaster the walls. However, when you are hungry, you'll eat anything. I did. I took any food that I could get my hands on.

When I had completed one month at the factory, I was required to go through another selection. The policemen told us to line up in two rows outside the building.

The bosses entered dressed in white coats. They looked like executioners. One walked behind the other, stopping, examining, scrutinizing each of us separately. They stopped in front of me; I couldn't say a word. I held my breath. Then they moved on. I thought I was safe. And then they started down the line again. They started pointing; first they chose that one, then another. Those people stepped out of line. When they did, one of the Jewish policemen took them aside. The chosen looked defeated, resigned to their fate. They shuffled their way out of the room like lambs being led to slaughter. The rest of us went back to work.

My friend and I exchanged notes on what was happening at work. He wasn't as lucky as I. He worked for Hering, the one who had the Music Room. Hering was known for his vicious attitude. He liked to kick people as he walked by. He also liked to hit women in the face, with a club or his fist. It didn't matter to him.

Another truck rolled into the yard. This group was from the town of Szydlowiec. How different they looked from us. They were clean; they looked like they had eaten regularly. In turn, my clothes were tattered; my underwear had fallen apart so I threw them away. There wasn't much left of my shoes. All I had to wear was pants and a jacket. Furthermore, my pants were too big. I held them up with a piece of rope around my waist. Once I had a leather belt, but I had traded it for a piece of bread. The buttons fell off my jacket, so I used another piece of rope to keep it shut. I was afraid that if I took another shower, they would delouse my clothes. Surely they would fall apart. Then what would I wear?

Next morning, the policeman came in screaming for everyone to get up. Usually they gave us half an hour to wash up and then we lined up in the square for work. This morning, Sigmund, the chief's assistant, came in and started swinging his rubber hose at everyone.

"Wake up. Wake up," he shouted. In five minutes everyone was up and out in the square lined up.

Members of the other barracks were lined up, too. A ripple of excitement ran through the camp. Soon the German commandant arrived. He was wearing a field officer uniform and on his belt hung a leather holster with a pistol. A German man was with him. His left hand was crippled and he covered it with a black leather glove. Since he had a defective trait, he was not allowed to be in the army. Men like him volunteered to help the war machinery for Hitler and were assigned to special duties. Two Ukrainians, with rifles, walked behind them. The Jewish commandant was also present.

He stood in front of the line and without a word stated to move down the line pointing at people. Each person who was pointed at was escorted out of line by a Jewish policeman. Then he stood in from of my friend and I. He pointed at us. My heart stopped. Both of us stood still, our eyes on the ground, not moving a muscle. Finally, the German stepped forward and grabbed my friend by the shirt and pulled him out of line. Relief flooded my soul. I was saved for another time, but my heart was breaking. Tears came to my eyes. He was my friend; he was just a kid. Why did they have to take him?

CHAPTER IX

Later in the day, we heard that a foreman from Hering's department had escaped during the night. Usually the people who escaped were caught and brought back to camp. They were always executed in front of the whole camp, although it was usually the night crew who had to watch. This man, whatever his name, was never seen or heard of again. Silently we cheered for him.

Things settled into a dull routine, work, nagging hunger and lice that were eating me alive. Winter was settling in. I had no socks and my feet were freezing. I found some old newspapers and wrapped my feet with them. I felt a little warmer. The only heat in the barracks came from a small potbelly stove in the center of the building. The Germans gave us no coal or wood. The only time we had a fire was when someone brought in wood from the factory. We'd shove and push to get close to the stove. Unfortunately, the fire went out so fast we wondered if it was worth lighting it. It was so cold I couldn't sleep. I would rather go to work in the factory which had central heating. At least it was warm there.

One day at lunch time, I was walking through the factory where the girls were packing the bullets that we were manufacturing. They packed the bullets in big boxes that were tied with cloth belts. I looked around to see if anyone was watching. Good! No one was looking. I pulled a belt off a box and threw the box in a corner. I pocketed the belt and went back to work. Later, back in the barracks, I studied the belt. It was made of very strong threads but loosely woven. I cut the buckle off with a makeshift knife (another broken law I had committed which was punishable by death of course) that I had traded for a piece of bread. I pulled the first thread. It came out easily. I tried to break the thread but couldn't.

I remembered an old shoemaker, in one of the other barracks. I went to see him.

"Is this any good?" I asked him. He looked at the ball of string in silence. Then he took out a piece of wax from the box he was sitting on and rubbed the thread with the wax.

"It's very good," he said. "I can use it. What is it worth to you?"

"Half a portion of bread?"

"Sold!" He dug in his box and took out a slice of bread. He cut it in half and held half out for me. "I will take as much string as you can get. I can use it for repairing shoes and boots." That made me happy.

"I will get more," I told him. "I will bring it all to you."

The next day I was able to get another belt. Days passed and each day I had another belt in my possession. Then one day the shoemaker told me.

"I have another person who brings me this thread from the belts. Would you believe it is a girl?" That made me nervous.

"I cannot get you anymore thread," I said. "I am afraid I will get caught."

The next three days I stood outside at the window during lunch time, watching to see who else was taking the belts. For several days I couldn't see who the culprit was. Then, just about the time I was going to give up, I saw the girl who cleaned the factory. She just walked into the room and started sweeping the floor. Unusual! She didn't like her job well enough to give up her lunch. She moved over the boxes, took a belt and hid it in the pocket of her apron. Then she looked around and pulled three belts off the boxes and put them in her pocket. What a hog! I only took one belt at a time. I decided to have a conversation with her.

"What are you going to do with the belts?" I asked. At first, she played dumb.

"What belts? I don't know what you are talking about."

"I saw you take them. I've been watching you."

"You're taking belts, too," she said to me.

"Look," I said. "I am not taking any more belts. They'll notice the belts are missing and if they catch us you know what they will do."

"You're right. We're fools to keep taking them," she answered. So we promised each other we wouldn't take any more belts after that night.

Nearing the gates of the camp, we saw the policemen searching everyone. I moved away from the girl. I wondered what they were searching for. What if they find the belts on her? Will she squeal on me? The policeman moved over to me and began going through my pockets. I had to open my jacket to show him I didn't have anything in them.

"What are you looking for?" I asked.

"Never mind," he said and pushed me inside the gate. I waited to see what would happen. I didn't have long to wait. The policeman took the girl away. To the police headquarters, I supposed. I was worried. I started to shake. When I entered the barracks someone asked me if I was sick.

"No," I said. "I'm all right." But I wasn't. I was sick with worry. What would they do to her? Would they beat her? Would she tell them about me?

Half an hour later, I was somewhat warm and feeling better. Suddenly, the door flew open. A policeman stood there.

"Henry Golde. Come forward. Follow me," he ordered.

"What is this all about? I asked.

"The Jewish Chief of Police wants to talk to you."

"About what?"

"I don't know," he answered.

There were six policemen sitting in chairs around the room. The Chief was sitting behind his big desk.

"Everyone, get out of the room, " he said. Then he looked at me. "And you! Pull up a chair in front of my desk. Sit down." When all the others had left the room and closed the door, he looked at me from behind his glasses. He just stared at me, then without saying a word he opened a drawer and pulled out the three belts, throwing them on the desk. I tried to keep a noncommittal expression on my face.

"Have you seen these belts before?" I pretended to inspect them very close.

"NO!" I answered. The Chief was quiet.

"Liar!" he suddenly burst out. He came around the desk and sat on top of the desk in front of me. "So you don't know anything about it?" His hand swung out and slapped me across the face so hard that I fell on the floor. I lay there for a minute. My ears were ringing.

"Get up," he yelled. I got up. "You still don't know anything?"

"No!" He smacked me in the face. Over and over again. I fell to the floor.

"Well, now maybe you will know something. Get up!"

I got up again feeling sick. I sat on the chair. He grabbed me by the front of my jacket, lifted me up with one hand and started slapping me with the other. He hit me with his open palm, first on one side, then on the other. He did this repeatedly. My face felt like an inflated balloon. Then he stopped smacking me and pushed me into the chair. I felt faint.

"We have the girl you know. We found the belts on her. She tells me you gave her the belts."

"No! I didn't. I never saw those belts before," I lied.

"Why does she say you gave her the belts, instead of someone else?"

"I don't know. I didn't give them to her."

"Do you know Krause asked me to find the person who has been stealing the belts. That when I do, I am to turn that person over to him?" I didn't say anything. "Do you know that is sabotage?" Again, I didn't answer. "Maybe I will hand you over to the Germans. They will get it out of you."

"I can't tell you something that I don't know anything about," I answered.

He kicked the chair out from under me and I ended up back on the floor. He started kicking me. I gritted my teeth and refused to cry. I hated the Germans so much they couldn't make me do anything I didn't want to do. Finally, he stopped.

"Okay, I will give you until morning to tell me. If you don't, I will hand you over to Krause. Now, get out." Then he gave me one more kick. I tried to get up, but I couldn't. The Chief lifted me up. "Next time it will be worse," he said. Leaving his office, I gave him the fiercest look of contempt I could muster.

"Do you want more of the same?" he asked. I turned and slowly walked out the door. My whole body was in pain. My face burned and it hurt to walk. I wondered if I had any broken bones. I went straight to the women's barracks. I was mad. I found the girl lying on her bunk. She looked pitiful. Her face was red and swollen. One of her eyes was puffed up so much, she could hardly see with it. She was crying. The anger left me. I felt sorry for her.

"Why did you tell them that I gave you the belts?"

"I don't know," she answered through her tears. "He beat me so bad I was all confused."

"I hope we both don't end up in the forest over this," I replied. "Did you say anything else to him?"

"No." Then I told her what had happened and that he gave me until tomorrow morning to talk.

"I won't tell him anything even if he kills me," I said.

"I'll tell him that I was the one who lied," she said.

"Well, I don't care what you tell him." With that I left. When I got back to my barracks some of the men asked me questions about what had happened to me. I didn't tell them anything. Two men helped me to my bunk. Another man brought me a damp rag to put on my face.

"You will feel better in the morning," he assured me.

I wondered. I'd probably get another beating like the one I had today. I fell asleep, but was awakened when a policeman came in screaming for everyone to get up. I was so sore I could barely get out of the bunk. In the washroom I bathed my face with cold water. It felt good on swollen face. I wiped my face with my filthy jacket sleeve. We lined up by the gate. The Chief stood their with the policeman. What would he do now? He just stood there. The policeman motioned for us to follow him. We started walking out the gate. No one made a move to stop me. I looked for the cleaning girl. She was there and fell in step with me.

"What happened," I asked.

"I went to him the first thing this morning and told him the truth. He said he wouldn't tell my boss, but if any more belts are missing, he would come after both of us." I sighed a huge sigh of relief.

CHAPTER X

Life went along at a normal pace, as normal as it could be. We lived with hunger, fear, bitterness and filth. It had become a way of life. We huddled by the potbelly stove night after night during the harsh winter. That is, as long as the fire lasted. We were grateful for the man who brought scrap wood home with him. Samuel, a man who slept several bunks down the other row, sometimes sang. He had a beautiful voice and we often joined in. He made up words. My favorite was:

> When does a Jew sing, when?
> When he is good and hungry
> He sings the song to forget it
> Humbala, humbala, humbalalaicia
> Humbala, humbala, humbalalaicia.

The song cheered us up. Any song cheered us! We forgot our troubles and developed a camaraderie among us. I always fell sleep easily after the songs, with hopes for a better tomorrow.

Snow had covered the ground and my clothes were nothing more than rags. I was constantly cold. Then, one day at work, Pavlowski pointed at me.

"He gets one," he said. Zosia, a Jewish supervisor, nodded her head.

"Yes sir," she answered.

I was very puzzled. What did it mean? Should I be happy or should I be frightened? What was I going to get? When the lunch bell rang, I ran to the lunch room as fast as I could.

"What am I supposed to get?" I asked her.

"When you get back to the camp tonight, you will come with me to the Jewish Commandant's office," she seemed pleased to tell me. "You will get a new suit and a new pair of shoes."

I couldn't wait. If I looked at the clock once, I looked twenty times. Finally, the shift whistle blew. I was the first one to get outside and the first in line to march to the camp.

"Could we please go get my suit?" I asked Zosia.

"I think you should wait until after supper," she said.

"No, no. I can't wait that long," I responded.

Evidently she was amused. We went directly to the commandant's office. The commandant looked at me and said, "Yes, if anyone needs new clothes, it is him."

They rummaged through piles of clothes looking for my size. All the clothes were navy blue and the material looked different than any material I had ever seen. I touched it; it was paper. If I hadn't hated the Germans so much, I would have given them more credit for their remarkable ingenuity. They made coffee out of beets, potatoes into potato flakes and now, suits made out of paper. The suit they gave me was too large. I rolled up the sleeves and then the pant cuffs. At first, the paper was stiff. I felt like a walking board. But, it was much nicer, much warmer than my old clothes.

"It's good," I told them. The shoes had wooden soles and leather tops. They were too big for me also, but I stuffed paper around my feet until I could walk without them flopping loosely.   The next day Pavlowski smiled as he walked over to me.

"Your new clothes? It is better, hey?" It was the first time he had ever smiled at me.

"Yes sir! Much better sir!" I answered.

The snow began to melt in spots. There were a few signs that spring was on the way, but not enough to warm the earth. In the next room where the girls examined the bullets, Pavlowski screamed.

"All you girls, line up. Get outside and line up. Now you lazy, good-for- nothing Jews, run, run, across the road to Hering's department."

We knew what that meant. The girls were going to the 'Music Room.' There would be beatings. I watched through the window. Pavlowski, his wife, Krause and Ladick stopped the girls outside the building. Hering went inside and came back out with a rubber hose. He turned the water on full force and aimed it at the girls.

They held up their arms and tried to shield their bodies. Then, because the ground was cold and icy, they fell slipping and sliding all the way to the earth. Then the bosses had the water shut off and started screaming at them.

"Get up you lazy swine. Get up."

Those who didn't or couldn't get up fast enough got kicked. The bosses then shoved and pushed and herded them like cows into the building. About an hour later, the girls came back out. Some had been beaten so badly, they had to be dragged out. Their faces were badly bruised; blood streaked down their faces and in their hair. Some of their clothing was torn and they walked miserably. I looked at Pavlowski. This was the same person who had given me a new suit of clothes?

We never learned why the girls had been punished. We helped them get back to the barracks after the shift was done. Some of the girls were never able to work again. They went to the forest. The remainder of the girls did not survive the next selection. I think they went to the forest, too.

I made it through the next selection. The new replacements arrived, this time they were from Krakow. Oh, they looked so healthy, so clean. I pitied them, for it would not last long. But maybe they would, for some of them smuggled in money. We had no idea how they got the money in, but they were able to buy good jobs with it. Some of them became Jewish policemen.

The camp was full of new people, but slowly things returned to normal. Gray days, sunny days, it made no difference. All the days were the same. Spring was coming, my thirteenth birthday wasn't far away. I wondered if I would see the fourteenth.

With spring came warm weather. I thought I would welcome the change of temperature, but the entire camp became muddy. Thick, slimy mud stuck to everything and tracked it all over the camp. It was hard to walk in mud that was five and six inches deep on the surface. It sucked at our feet and we had to constantly pull our feet up forcefully. Another thing that changed with warm weather was the lice. They bit harder and more often. I scratched, and scratched, and scratched. Sometimes I scratched myself raw.

I still snuck into the kitchen for bits and scraps to eat. I felt like

a dog, but my hunger drove me to go back to the kitchen over and
over again.

One day the big machine broke down. Pavlowski told me to
switch off my machine. That was fine with me; I was way ahead of
production anyway. So I switched it off and sat down behind my
machine. Unfortunately, I dozed off. I awoke with someone poking
me in the ribs. I opened my eyes to see an Ukrainian guard standing over me, poking me with his rifle. I jumped up and faced him.
The guard started talking to me in Russian. I did not understand
what he was saying. I did get the drift that it was against the law to
fall asleep on the job.

"My machine broke down. I was waiting for it to be fixed. I
didn't mean to fall asleep," I said. He paid no attention and
motioned for me to come with him. Reluctantly, I followed. Zosia
came over to us. She tried to explain the circumstances. He would-
n't listen to any words of excuse.

"Come," he muttered and pushed me out of the factory. I followed him down the road that led to the Ukrainian headquarters. It
was a small building next to the gate of the factory. I was begging
and pleading with him. "Keep walking," he said.

I was frightened. I was more scared than I had ever been before.
I had heard others talk of what went on here. The Ukrainians took
people in their headquarters and beat them to a pulp. I feared my
fate, but I resigned myself. What is going to happen is going to
happen, I told myself.

He opened the door and with a flourish indicated that I should
enter. In the middle of the room was a large table with a group of
men, all Ukrainians, playing cards. No one looked up when we
walked in. The guard who had escorted me to their headquarters
put his rifle in a corner. He pulled up a chair and spoke loudly.

"Isn't anyone going to help me?" he asked.

"Why? What have you got there?"

"I found this loafer sleeping on the job. That is a very serious
mistake."

"Yah!" said another. "That is very bad."

"I will help," came another voice looking me over. They got up
from the table and went to the wall where there were various sized

tree clubs. They approached me menacingly.

"Bend over the chair. I obeyed.

"Start counting," someone said.

The first blow went through my body like a bolt of lightening. Anger boiled up, indignation raged through my body. I will not cry, I will not cry, I will not scream, I kept saying to myself silently. I started to count the blows with them partially to show how brave, how determined, I was and partially to skip a few numbers, confuse them, and perhaps not take so many blows. It didn't work. They simply started counting from the beginning. My back felt like it had been through a meat tenderizer. They kept taking turns wielding the clubs. When they were done, I was so sore I could hardly get up. Somehow I managed.

"Run," they told me. I tried, but the door was miles away from my grasp. I thought I was going to faint.

Whack! A club found a place to land along side my head. But I was still standing. Then one of them tripped me and I fell. They roared with laughter. They leaned over me and the blows came fast and furious. Somehow, some way, I managed to get up, struggled to reach the door. It was locked. Laughter, not mine, rang through the room. Through blood dripping down my face, I saw the key. I managed to turn it and got the door open. I must have stumbled. Maybe I was pushed outside, I can't remember.

Eventually, I made my way to the factory. The big machine still wasn't working. I tried to sit down, but couldn't. My back felt like raw meat. My head hurt; the room started spinning around. I fainted. Zosia was looking at me from a very high place, at least she looked very far away. She was holding my head and had a glass of water in her hand. She splashed water on my face and insisted I sip some.

"Help me up," I asked. "Please, help me." She started to help me just when Pavlowski approached us.

"What goes on here? What has happened to this boy?" Zosia explained everything. "I will go down there and talk with those Ukrainian pigs," Pavlowski said.

Two men helped me get back to the barracks. They also lifted me up on my bunk. My back was so painful I couldn't lie on it. It felt like it was burning with hot coals. Some men brought wet cloths and placed them on my back. Someone else took my container and filled it with soup and gave me my ration of bread for the day. It was agony to sit up just to drink my soup. However, the next morning I knew it was either work or the forest. I got up and went to work.

Pavlowski came over to me. "How do you feel?"

"Fine," I answered.

"Good! Don't worry. They will not bother you again." It was a full two weeks before I could sit or lay on my back. I was told my back was black as coal. It felt much worse than that.

A small transport arrived from Warsaw. This time the newcomers didn't look clean, nicely dressed or healthy. On the contrary, they looked tired, drawn and haggard. Some of them even looked worse that we oldtimers. The new arrivals told us about the uprising in the Warsaw ghetto.

"Thousands are starving to death. There is no food, no water and no doctors. There is no anything. Just room for them to die," they were telling us. "Train loads of Jews have been taken to Treblinka. What? You haven't heard of Treblinka? It is the worst place to go. It is for extermination of all Jews. The Germans bring Jews in by the carloads. Men, women and children, it makes no difference. They tell them to go take showers, but they aren't showers. Instead they are gas chambers. They bury them in one huge, open pit."

Each story was filled with more sorrow and horror than the last. Or so I thought until I ran into a former neighbor who had been a friend of the family and later transported to Chmielnik.

"Henry. Oh Henry! I am so sorry to tell you this. Your Mother and your brother, Marcus. They are both gone. Marcus did come back from the work camp, but then they were taken with the rest of the people to Treblinka. It was not easy for them. It was not easy for anyone."

I sat alone in sorrow. What was left in this world for me? I had no one. I had no home. Only this camp! I would work until I couldn't work any more. Then what would happen? Would they take me to the forest? Probably! Then I thought of Mother and

Marcus. How handsome and strong he had been. I wished that I could have been with my mother and brother at the end, for nothing else but to say goodbye. To tell them how much I loved them both, and how proud I was of them. I didn't want to be here alone. I was only thirteen, but I felt like an old man. I was so sad, so lonely, so torn apart that I wanted to die. I was just a kid, and all alone.

CHAPTER XI

Life in the concentration camp went on, the daily struggle to stay alive. Some people had just given up. It was easy. Don't go to work for two days and you would be taken to the forest.

There was a doctor in camp now. He came with the transport from Krakow. They gave him his own office but no medicine or medical supplies of any kind. A lot of good he did here! At work there was a rumor that our department would be closed. There was also a rumor that the war with Russia wasn't going too well, which was why they would close our department. The powder was needed for real bullets, not blanks. One of the bosses, Krowser, was leaving to join the army. The next to go was Herring. He wouldn't be missed.

A week later, Pavlowski announced the department would close and all of the people would go to factory A. However, a few would stay and work at taking apart the blanks. That department would be run by his wife. She picked out twenty young boys and ten young women from different departments, including me. I felt good about it because the people who were transferred to work at factory A, would still stay at camp B. That meant going to work every day, five miles away, and then making the long trip back home at night.

The factory was rearranged and we were given small machines that pulled out the wooden tips and were operated by hand. Two people worked at each machine. One fed the bullets into the machine, and the other put a clamp on and pressed the handle, pulling the wooden tip out of the bullet. Then, the first person took the bullet out, emptied the powder into a wooden box, and threw the empty shell into another box. The operation looked easy, but, sometimes, when the bullet wasn't perfectly in the middle, the wooden tip cracked and wouldn't come out. When that happened, a pair of pliers was used to try to pull out the tip.

Our new lady boss chose a foreman, an older man who was responsible for us. A policeman was also assigned to our group, the friend of my brother from back home. He took us to work, got the soup and distributed it during lunch and supper and brought in the night shift and escorted the day shift back to the barracks.

Our work wouldn't be too hard, except the boss put a quota on each shift. The quota was impossible to make; therefore, every morning the day shift was taken to a small room before work and our policeman dished out the punishment with the club. The night shift got the same treatment.

I wasn't sure why I didn't like that woman before. Now I knew – she was a sadist. She watched while the policeman beat us and I watched her. There was pure pleasure in her face, especially if someone cried out during the beatings. The louder the screams, the more her enjoyment. Why did she pick only the young boys and girls? She hated the Jews, but hated Jewish kids even worse. The rumor was that before she married, she was a prostitute and had her tubes tied. Now she couldn't have any children. Well, maybe that was only a rumor. Who knows?

Our foreman didn't escape the beatings. The only difference was his was done in private, after everyone else got theirs. We go over to work and he gets worked over. I was the one she really didn't like. I upset her because I never cried when I got a beating. I seemed to always have a sarcastic smile on my face when I looked at her. I didn't even realize I was doing it; it just happened. I guess all the contempt I felt for these people had to surface. That smile cost me plenty. First, when the policeman gave out second servings of soup. She told him I didn't get any more. When I was beaten and the policeman didn't hit me too hard or too long then told me to go. She had him beat me again, harder, so I really got it twice. But I gritted my teeth, probably sneering in the process. I don't know, but I never uttered a sound.

One night a young boy told the policeman that he had a boil on his buttock and pleaded with him not to hit him. The boss told the boy to pull down his pants so she could see it. The boy let down his pants and, sure enough, one side of his buttock had a big boil. The whole area was inflamed. She told the policeman to hit him on the other side and the boy screamed in pain. I could hear the boy, but I was looking at her. Her face was lit up with excitement. She loved it. What made that woman so sadistic? I hoped that some day she'd get what was coming to her.

One day she called me into her office. There was a Polish woman working for her. As I walked in, they were talking and laughing about something. The boss turned around and faced me. In her hand she held a very thin twig, which she started tapping on my head.

"See, he is laughing at me again," she said to the other woman. Then she said to me, "Why do you laugh at me?"

"I can't help myself," I answered. "I don't even know I'm doing it." In the meantime, she was tapping away at my head. It smarted.

"I'll wipe that smile off your face yet," she said as she glared at me. I guess I had become a challenge to her. She cracked me across the face with the twig. Oh, how it stung, but I didn't make a sound. "Get out of here," she said angrily. I turned and left the office, touching my burning face.

When I got to work, the girl who worked with me said, "That's a nasty welt you have there. You better go to the washroom and put some water on it." I did and, oh, the water felt good on my face. I'd better try to stop smiling at that bitch before she killed me. But the next time we saw each other at lunch time, and I did the same thing.

"No extra soup for him," she ordered.

On the way home that evening, our policeman talked to me.

"Why are you doing this to her? Why are you laughing at her? She will kill you. She is capable of doing it and I don't want to see that happen to you. After all, I feel responsible for you, you being from my home town." That was my brother's good friend talking.

When I first came here, he had promised to help me. A lot of help I got from him! This was the first time he had spoken to me since my arrival. Was this what he called help? He lived pretty well in the factory. I understood that he couldn't give me any extra soup because the boss was watching. When she was there, he gave any leftover soup to all the workers, except for me. When she wasn't watching, he took the rest of the soup and traded for different things or sold it for money, if anyone had any. If there was still some soup left over, the policeman ate it. This went on throughout the camp. My brother's friend never offered me anything. He could have, but he didn't.

Each policeman had a girlfriend. These girls were well taken care of and wanted for nothing. But one night, a girl was found in our barracks on a man's bunk. The Police Chief dragged her out and gave her such a beating that he broke her jaw. Later that week, she was taken into the forest. Another time they found a woman who was pregnant and she, too, was taken into the forest. Who would think that under these circumstances, sex would play such a big role? But it did.

For a change, I liked working the night shift every second week. When I was on the night shift, I slept in the morning, and in the afternoon I went to the commandant's office to ask him if he had any odd jobs for me to do. Some days he invited me in to clean his room and, for that, he gave me a piece of bread. However, there were some drawbacks to being in the barracks during the day. If the German or Ukrainians wanted anything special done, the Jewish police came to get us whether we were sleeping or not. We did that job and in the evening we had to go to our regular jobs in the factory, tired or not.

Also, when there was an execution in camp, it was done during the day. Sleeping or not, we were dragged out to watch.

One day the Germans and Ukrainians brought a man and a woman into camp, a husband and wife brought here on the transport from Krakow. The Jewish policeman woke everyone up and chased us outside. I saw this couple in the middle of the square, looking like they had been badly beaten. There were a few Ukrainians and the German commandant, and also a man dressed in civilian clothes wearing a long black coat and a black felt hat. He was, I found out, the dreaded Gestapo. The Jewish policeman walked briskly over to the German commandant and told him everyone was accounted for. The German began screaming about those two scum who tried to escape.

"You will soon see what is going to happen to them and anyone else who tries to escape. Tomorrow twenty of you lousy dogs are going to be selected and shot. You can thank those two lousy dogs for that," he shouted. He walked over to the couple and slapped the man in the face. "On your knees, you dog." The man obeyed. The German hit the man's wife in the face and told her to go down on her knees. He kicked the man in the back and ordered,

"Embrace that whore." The man put his arms around his wife. He tried to kiss her but their lips were so swollen and cut they barely touched. In their eyes I could see that they were resigned to their fate. They knew they would be shot. They seemed to be saying goodbye to each other without saying a word.

The Germans and Ukrainians seemed to enjoy the whole scene. I saw excitement in their faces. The German commandant took his pistol from its holster, put the barrel to the woman's temple, and a shot rang out. Her body went limp in her husband's arms. She was dead. It looked like half her head was blown away. She was covered with blood and so was her husband, but he still held her in his arms, crying silently. The commandant put his arm down, still holding the pistol.

"Well dog, how do you like your whore now?" he said to the man. Still holding his wife's body, he cried out.

"Please shoot me, shoot me."

The German, ignoring the man's pleas, addressed us.

"Now you see? He wants to be shot. You dirty Jews are all alike. The glorious Third Reich is good enough to give you work, food, and shelter and you are not satisfied. You want to escape. This is what you are going to get if you try to escape."

With that, he put his pistol to the man's temple. Another shot rang out and both bodies fell to the ground in a heap. The German commandant told the Jewish commandant,

"Clean that shit up."

"Yes sir," replied the Jewish commandant as he jumped to attention. "Okay," he shouted, "dismissed." We started back to the barracks. The two Germans left, talking to each other between their laughing. The Ukrainians who followed looked very indifferent to the whole situation. I stood there staring at the bodies feeling numb, as if in a trance. Finally, someone pushed me lightly on the shoulder.

"Come, now. It's all over," he said. I snapped out of it and looked up at the man who had spoken. He, too, had sadness in his eyes. "We can't help them now. It's all over." He took me by the shoulders and led me back to the barracks.

It was quiet inside. Everyone was lying on their bunks, deep in their own thoughts. I was lying on my bunk and staring up at the ceiling. All I could think of was the lousy bastards, the lousy bastards. Where is God? Where is God? There is no God, there can't be.

Life went on in camp. Sometimes I felt like this was a dream, a terrible nightmare, and any moment I would wake up and be back home with my family, and everything would be all right. I wondered if there were any kids like me anywhere in the world who lived under normal conditions, in homes, with their families, happy, not worrying about survival like I was. Not having to worry about sleeping in a warm bed, with covers, or when and if your next meal would come. Here I was, in what the world would soon come to know as the worst prison in Poland, a nobody. I didn't think anyone even knew about us, or really cared. I felt like an old man, not at all like a thirteen-year-old, and I wondered, why? Why me? I tried to resign myself to my fate, but I kept plugging on.

One evening after work, we lined up as usual to be counted, then go home. This particular night some of the kids were still inside straightening up some of their work. Our policeman was in a big hurry to get back to camp. I didn't know why; maybe he had a date with his girlfriend, but he screamed at everyone to line up fast, and apparently I wasn't fast enough. He came over and smacked me in the face.

I was stunned. I had been slapped and beaten before and I never cried, but this time I did. When Jarmolaf, the Jewish police commandant, beat me senseless, I didn't cry. When the Ukrainian took me to their headquarters and beat me, I didn't cry. This time I was crying. The hurt wasn't as bad as the other times; I just never expected that this man, my brother's friend, would do that to me. Back home, when he and my brother were friends, he used to come to our apartment to visit. He knew me and my whole family. We, in turn, knew his. Now this man had smacked me.

I couldn't stop crying all the way to the barracks. That night, as I lay on my bunk, I started to cry again. I felt so let down. He was my last hope, the only one left who I thought was my friend. He had promised me, the first night I arrived in this hellhole, that he would take care of me. Since then, I had always thought that if I really needed someone I could turn to him. Now, I knew that I was all alone. I would have no one to turn to if the worst would come.

At work, things were coming to an end. We were finishing up the last boxes of bullets and everyone in the department started to worry. What would happen to us when we finished? What did our boss have in store for us? Would she send us to the forest? Maybe some of us. If she had the choice, I was sure to go; she never did like me. We would soon find out.

When the work was done that evening, the boss was nowhere around and we went back to camp. Before the policeman dismissed us, he started to call out names. Starting tomorrow, some of us would work at Laidik's department and some would go to factory A. I was going to Laidik. I had heard stories about that place: the work wasn't easy and most people had to do piece-work. If they couldn't produce, they were taken out and beaten. I also heard about the Polish foremen, that they were bastards. They lived in town and came to work in the morning and, at night, they returned to their own homes. I was worried that night. Was I going to fit into the new department? It really was better than going every day to factory A.

The next day I went into the new department. A Polish foreman, a young man about eighteen, put me at a machine and showed me what to do. This department had two big rooms. In the first room was a big cutting machine which cut steel tubing fed by one man. Oil spattered all over him and his skin was dark from the stains. He was also covered with small boils and blemishes. Those who worked this machine didn't last very long. One would get sick and another took his place.

The pieces of steel were cut to a certain length, then fed into a smaller machine which closed one end and shaped it to look like a bullet shell. The finished product was sent to the next room, which had many smaller machines that polished the shells. At the far end of the room, were small tables where women examined each shell. The machine I operated was a polishing machine, but not fully automatic. I had to use two levers and a foot pedal. I was given a pair of gloves because the steel got hot in the machine and I could burn my hands taking them out. There was also a glass shield between me and the machine because slivers of steel flew around as I polished the tubing. Sometimes the slivers burned any skin that wasn't covered by the gloves.

It took quite a few days to learn the operation of the machine; I either polished the shells too much, or not enough. The foreman kept a close eye on me and always found something wrong with what I was doing, then pushed me around. Sometimes Laidik, the big boss, came through the building. He was a big man, very tall and fat. When he opened his mouth, it sounded like a lion's roar. If he didn't like someone, he killed him, and that happened daily. He almost always found something wrong, then screamed about it. One had to get out of his way or get kicked or punched. Sometimes he ordered the Polish foreman to take everyone out of the room and beat them with a club.

Wherever you saw Laidik, you saw his secretary. She was a very beautiful Polish girl. There was a rumor she was also his girlfriend. One day Laidik decided he wanted a swimming pool. Who was going to do the work? The slaves, the Jews. He ordered the foreman to give him twenty men to dig the hole by hand with shovels. I was surprised he didn't order them to dig with their bare hands.

Every few days, some of the men couldn't do the work anymore and had to be replaced. One day, I was sent there by my Polish foreman after he got mad at me and a few others. By the time I got there, the hole was about four feet deep. There were wooden planks laid from the bottom of the hole to the top and men working all over the place. Some were loading the wheelbarrows with the dirt they dug up and some were pushing them to the top and dumping the dirt on a big pile near the hole. We had a Jewish foreman for this job and he was responsible to Laidik for the work that was expected to be done. The foreman pleaded with everyone to work faster because when Laidik came around, which was at least once a day, and he felt more work should have been done, he started screaming and everyone got a beating, even the foreman got his share. He didn't like that.

The foreman gave me a shovel and, because of my size, told me to load the wheelbarrows. So far the dirt had been pretty soft and digging was easy. Soon I got to the gravel, which was harder to dig and much harder to lift on the shovel. In some places, there were big rocks. We were told that if there were any big rocks, they had to be dug up and brought to the top by using long sticks and pushing them, bit by bit. The whole scene looked like something from biblical times when the Jews had to build the pyramids in Egypt. At the end of the day, I was very tired and my back felt like it was breaking. Sometimes it seemed that working in the hole was nothing but some cruel punishment and the hole would never be finished.

One afternoon, another man and I had just finished loading a wheelbarrow. A third man took the wheelbarrow and pushed it to the top of the planks. There was a knack to it: he must push hard enough to get a fast start up the planks or he would never make it to the top. While he did that, we rested a bit on our shovels until he came back with the empty wheelbarrow and the operation started all over again. As we waited, we didn't realize that Laidik was standing on the ledge of the hole, along with his secretary, looking at us. He didn't approve of anyone not working, no matter what the reason. By the time we realized he was there, it was too late. He screamed for the foreman to come up. We feverishly started digging, hoping he really hadn't see us resting. The foreman stood in front of Laidik, who screamed at him at the top of his lungs. How useless he was for allowing the dirty dogs to stand around and loaf. From the corner of my eye, I watched. Laidik smacked him in the face again and again, then told the foreman to put us two on the wheelbarrow. We were in for it.

The foreman ran down and instructed us to man the wheelbarrow. I asked the man who was loading mine not to fill it too much, and he didn't. I picked up the wheelbarrow handles and started pushing up. Don't stop now, I told myself. I was halfway to the top but slowing down. Don't stop, don't stop. I knew I wouldn't make it. Another few steps and I lost the balance, and the wheelbarrow tipped over and wound up back in the hole. I tried to go after it, but Laidik started screaming. I got confused, not knowing what he wanted from me. The foreman ran over and said Laidik wanted me to come up. Hesitantly, I climbed to the top. All the while Laidik was screaming and calling me all kinds of pet names like Jew dog, lousy Jew, and whatever else he could think of. I looked up at him, a giant of a man. He slapped me in the face. I fell to the ground with him standing over me still screaming.

I lay there, unable to understand what he was saying. He kicked me in the ribs. I knew I'd better get up before he trampled me to death. Before I could get to my feet, he kicked me again. I saw his secretary trying to stop him.

"Leave him alone," she said. "He's only a kid. Please, leave him alone." But he wouldn't listen to her. Laidik slapped me again and again, all the time still screaming. He finally pushed me into the hole. Luckily I fell on loose dirt, which softened my fall, so I didn't get hurt much.

Laidik and his secretary left. The foreman helped me to my feet. I was beginning to feel more and more like a punching bag. The foreman put me back on digging and loading. The rest of the day I couldn't help thinking about what would happen to the foreman and me if Laidik came back and found me doing my original job, not the one he assigned me to. What would he do to the foreman, to me? I had a feeling that the next time he came around, that would be the end of me. To my relief, he didn't come back the rest of that day.

I got back to camp that evening feeling very sore. My ribs were bruised and they hurt again. My face hurt a little, but I guess my face was getting used to being slapped. All night I couldn't help wondering about the next day – would it be my last? I knew Laidik was going to kill me, but I also knew I must go to work tomorrow. Two days in the barracks and it was off to the forest. Well, what will be will be.

As I woke in the morning, I heard a big commotion. The night shift had just come home and they were talking very excitedly about Laidik. I jumped off the bunk and asked the first man I came to.

"What happened?"

"Laidik is dead," he said. I couldn't believe it.

"Yes, it's true. It happened last night at his secretary's apartment in town. The Polish Partisans walked in, took him to the forest, and riddled him with bullets, then hung his body on a tree on the way to the factory. The secretary disappeared. The Gestapo is looking for her." We found out later that she was working with the Polish underground movement and had used him the whole time. She had had him killed. I couldn't help thinking about what had happened the day before, but why? Why did she have him killed last night? Was it that she couldn't take it anymore? Was I responsible for it? Whatever the reason, to me it was like a miracle. Was there really a God in heaven? Did He help save my life? I suppose He was there, at least part of the time. I thanked Him for saving my life.

The next day, work on the swimming pool was stopped and the men were transferred back to the factory department. A new boss took over. He wasn't as ruthless as Laidik. I was back at the same machine with the same Polish foreman. He hadn't changed either, ever so often he would check on me and I would get pushed around.

Things got back to normal. Same hunger, occasional beatings, and living in filth. But something new was added in camp, air raids and blackouts at night. An order went out that during a blackout, no one was allowed to leave the barracks. The news was that the Germans weren't doing well on the Russian front.

One night I woke up with very bad cramps and had to go to the toilet. It was the middle of the night and everyone was snoring. As I went outside, half asleep, I didn't realize it was pitch dark. Usually the camp was well lit. The toilet was in a corner of the camp. I relieved myself and, feeling better, went outside to return to the barracks and ran into a barrel of a rifle. It belonged to an Ukrainian guard. He asked me if I didn't know I wasn't supposed to go outside during a blackout. I told him in my broken Russian that I didn't realize there was a blackout.

The moon was out and gave a little light. I could see him more clearly now. He was young, tall and fairly good-looking. I wanted to ask him what he would have me do, shit in my pants? But I didn't dare. He told me the penalty for going outside in a blackout was

death. I was to be shot. My knees went weak. He told me to turn
around and lift my arms, and without hesitation I did.

"Now, walk to the barbed wire fence," he said and I did. When
I got there he told me to stop, and I did. Facing the fence, I heard
him behind me, loading his rifle. So this it, I thought, this is the
end. This is the end of my miserable life. It had to come sometime.
Maybe it was better this way. I knew I would never come out of this
nightmare alive. No more hunger pains. No more filth and lice.
No more beatings. No more fighting to stay alive. One bullet and I
am dead. Would it hurt? Maybe he would miss me. No, please, I
screamed in silence. I don't want to die. I'm just a kid. Maybe I
should run. Maybe I can get away. It's dark. If I ran, he might not
see me and I could get away. No, he would come after me in the
barracks. No, there is no way out. I will die. Resign yourself.

All of these things were running through my mind. How long
had I been standing there? It couldn't be more than a few seconds,
yet it seemed like a lifetime. Now I knew what that couple had
gone through before they were shot. Suddenly, I heard footsteps and
strained to see who was coming. The figure of a man was coming
toward us. The guard saw him, too, and waited for him. It was
another Ukrainian guard, coming down the pass by the fence. I was
a little disappointed. Now both of them were going to have a little
fun with a Jew kid. Would they both shoot me? At the same time?
They exchanged greetings. The new guard asked the first one what
he was doing. He told him how I broke the law by going outside in
a blackout and that he was going to shoot me. I caught a glimpse of
the new guard from the corner of my eye. We was a much older
man. He told the first guard to leave me alone. Did I dare hope?

"No, I will shoot him," he insisted. I knew it. I'm dead.

"Leave him alone. He's only a kid," the older guard repeated in a
strong voice. My arms were still in the air; they felt like lead, but I
was afraid to put them down. Who would win this argument?
How cheap my life was. It was hanging on a thread in the hands of
these two Ukrainian peasants. I felt like screaming 'go ahead, shoot!
Get it over with. I can't take it anymore.' But I stood there not
moving, with my arms in the air, while these two argued about me.
The older one said he would take over.

"You are off duty. You leave him to me. Go home, you must be tired." The other one didn't answer. "Go ahead, go."

"Okay, I'm going," he answered and walked away muttering to me, "You Jew son-of-a-bitch." I thought to myself, drop dead, you bastard. I put my arms down; I couldn't keep them up anymore. "Go ahead, kid. Get out of here," the guard told me as he nudged me in the side with his rifle. He didn't have to say that twice. Even though my knees were wobbly, I ran all the way to the barracks. I couldn't sleep the rest of the night, thinking about my latest experience. There must be a God in heaven. He saved my life again. But why? Why me? Others were dying like flies. My family was killed. Why? Because we are God's chosen people, I remembered my father telling me Ha!, I got saved again, but this was torment. I didn't tell anyone what had happened to me because nobody would care anyway. It was every dog for himself and no one on the outside cared what the Germans did to us. They turned us into animals. Animals cared only about food and survival, and we did, too.

A few weeks later in the middle of the night, we were awakened by someone screaming for us to get outside, now. Everyone jumped out of their bunks and ran for the door. An Ukrainian guard was doing the screaming, pushing everyone through the door with his rifle butt. When we were outside, he told us to run to one end of the camp. When we got there, he told us to run to the other side. Back and forth we ran. After we did this ten times, he ordered us back to the barracks. While running, a few men got hit by his rifle.

A couple of them were badly hurt. What was the reason for this? Was he bored and figured he would have some fun with the Jews? No one knew, or at least no one talked about it. I guess we all took this kind of thing for granted and, of course, we were glad it wasn't worse. They were the masters and could do anything they wanted – the Germans, the Ukrainians, the Polish foremen, and the Jewish police. They were our masters. We were the slaves and must obey, without question.

One day while I was working on the machine, a steel sliver hit my ankle. It burned a little, but I didn't pay too much attention to it. A few days later, my ankle started to feel uncomfortable; in fact, it hurt. It was swollen and starting to fester. I had difficulty standing or walking on that foot. It wasn't getting any better, so one evening I went to the Jewish doctor in camp. He looked at it and shook his head, and told me he couldn't do anything for me because he didn't have any medicine. The only thing to do without proper medicine, he said, was for me to urinate on it. That would stop the infection. At first I thought he was crazy, but I figured I had nothing to lose. By now, the wound was wide open to where you could see the ankle bone, full of puss and inflamed. I followed the doctor's orders and started to urinate on it and it felt a little better. It was agony for me to stand all day on that foot, but I knew I couldn't stay in the barracks. I had to go to work.

At this time, the camp was going through the beginning of an epidemic of typhoid fever. To combat the disease, the Germans built a special barracks right outside the camp gates. Whoever was suspected of having the dreaded typhoid was transferred to this barracks, which was laughingly called 'the hospital.' Those who were transferred there were not treated, but were left to die. They either died in the so-called hospital, or occasionally a truck would arrive to take them to the forest to be shot. That was probably the only humane thing they did without realizing it was humane. Shooting them took them out of their misery a little faster.

Every day the pile of bodies outside the hospital grew. This was their burial ditch. When someone in the hospital died, their body was thrown on the pile. Later, the bodies would be put on a truck and dumped in the forest. Every time I went through the gate and saw this pile, I couldn't help thinking that even the dead Jews didn't get any respect. The bodies looked like garbage dumped from a pail.

Once, I witnessed the truck being loaded. Two men would grab a body by the arms and legs and throw it up on the truck, while the uniformed German truck driver nonchalantly smoked a cigarette until the truck was loaded. Who were these people they were throwing on the truck? Didn't they have a name? Wasn't anyone keeping track? Did anyone care?

Surprisingly, my foot was getting better, but one night I was burning with fever. In the morning, I couldn't get out of the bunk to go to work. I had prayed all through the night that I wouldn't have typhoid fever. I kept telling myself that the fever was from my ankle and that it would get better.

After the counting of the heads before work, a Jewish policeman came into the barracks and called my name. I answered. He came over to my bunk and asked what was wrong with me. I told him my ankle bothered me and I couldn't go to work today, but tomorrow I would be fine. It seemed to be all right with him that I didn't go work that day, but as he left the barracks he informed me he would send the doctor to look at me. That's exactly what I didn't want him to do. I tried to convince myself that the fever was from the infection in my ankle, but deep down I knew it was from typhoid. I was burning up, but the last thing I wanted was to go to the hospital.

An hour later the doctor came in to look at me. He put his hand on my forehead, took my pulse, and confirmed my fear. I had typhoid fever and he was going to put me in the hospital. That hit me worse than the physical beatings I had gotten so far. For sure, this was the beginning of the end. Much too soon two men came in and helped me off my bunk, propped me up and helped me walk to the hospital barracks. I didn't realize how weak I really was. Without their help, I could never have made it.

Typhoid fever strikes fast. Once you contact the disease, the fever gets higher and higher and within forty-eight hours, if your body can't ward it off, you die. Or, if you're fortunate, the fever breaks and you're on the road to recovery. In the hospital barracks, I assessed the situation. I was getting good at that; one quick glance and I already knew where things stood. There was one big room with bunks on each side and an aisle in the middle. Each bunk was free-standing with a little space between each one. All were occupied except for two at the end of the room. They helped me into one of them.

This was no good, no good at all, I'm through. When the barracks got full, that meant only one thing: the Germans would come with their truck and take everyone out to the forest to make room for another batch. I had such a hopeless feeling in the pit of my stomach. There was nothing I could do; I was dead either way. If the fever didn't get me, the Germans would. I looked around at the people and watched them twist and turn in their bunks. Some of them looked unconscious.

I was burning all over. Funny, I didn't feel hungry. I couldn't remember the last time I didn't feel hungry, but I was thirsty. I could drink anything I could get my hands on. Two men walked around the room, looking at the people in their bunks. They stopped by one where a woman lay dying.

"She's dead. We better get her out of here," said one of the men. They took her by the hands and feet and dragged her limp body out of the barracks. Is that what they were going to do with me? I wondered who the woman was. She must have had a family, but here there was no one to mourn for her. If she had any family, they were probably dead. Her body must be lying on top of the pile now, like a piece of garbage. What an end to a person's life. God, did she deserve this? Not even a decent burial. She probably never did anything wrong in her life. There was no answer to this.

The two men returned and continued walking among the bunks, looking and listening. They reminded me of a couple of vultures waiting for their prey to die. One of them came over to me and asked If I would like something.

"Yes, please, some water," I said. "I'm so thirsty." He said he would bring me some water but it would cost me my portion of bread. You bastard, I thought. Even when you're looking at human misery, you only think of yourself. I had no choice but to agree. He would have stolen the bread from me anyhow. He took my container and soon came back with water. I drank the water like a man lost in a desert. Now, I felt a little better and fell asleep.

I must have slept for hours. When I woke up, it was dark outside and the lights were on in the barracks. I looked around, at first not knowing where I was. The same people were still turning and tossing around, while others screamed for water. The two men who worked here were sitting at the front of the barracks, ignoring the people's cries for help and water. I was able to stretch my neck and see that a few more bunks were empty. Those people must have died while I was asleep. Is this what I have to look forward to? Go to sleep and never wake up?

I was burning again and my head was pounding. Thirsty, I looked in my container and found a little water left. I gulped it down and fell asleep again. I woke up once more during the night, unable to lift my head. My whole body felt like it was on fire. I was so thirsty I wanted to scream for water, but no words would come out. I fell asleep again.

In the morning, I awoke to a commotion. Turning my head toward the door, I saw the German and Jewish commandants. Behind them was the Ukrainian guard. The two Jewish men who worked in the hospital were taking people out of their bunks and carrying them outside. This is it, I thought. This is for sure the end. It won't be long now. Maybe it's better this way. At least no more waiting and wondering. I'll be out of my misery, once and for all. Go ahead, take me.

The group was moving slowly, stopping at every bunk. As the German motioned with his hand, the two men grabbed the person in the usual manner and out they went. They were coming closer to my bunk. The man next to me was carried out. I felt myself entering unconsciousness. Through a fog, I saw the German in front of my bunk and I heard him.

"What about this little guy?" he asked. Off in the distance came the answer.

"He's getting better already. He will be out of here tomorrow."

"Okay, leave him alone," the German said and they turned and left the barracks. The Jewish commandant saved my life. Why?

I didn't know how long I was unconscious, but when I woke up I felt better. I wasn't burning like I was before. Slowly, everything came back to me. I lifted myself on my elbows and looked around. I saw only two bunks occupied. I called to one of the attendants.

"You're better," he told me. "You have beaten the fever." I guess I did! I was hungry and I asked for some soup. He told me the soup wouldn't be ready for an hour and that I would have to wait. "You're lucky. You're the only one they didn't take out."

I didn't know that. I asked how long I'd been unconscious and he said a day and a half. I lay back, feeling like I just went through a wringer. I ran my hand over by body; it felt like a bag of bones. I felt my ankle and it was better, too. The wound had closed and it didn't throb anymore. Another miracle? Maybe there was someone up there looking out for me. What for? More misery? Hadn't I been punished enough for whatever crime I had committed?

During the next few days I spent in the hospital barracks, I was getting stronger and thinking about food, a good sign my health was improving. I could walk around the barracks now. It was getting full again; I'd better get out of here before the Germans came back to clean house. This time they might take me, too, just for their own pleasure.

The next day I asked one of the men to let me go back to camp. The two of them discussed it and finally agreed to let me go. One of them escorted me out of the hospital, but said we must report to the Jewish commandant. At his office, my escort told him that I was well and ready to go back to work.

"Good," the commandant said. "You will stay in camp for a couple days before I send you back to work." I tried to argue that I was ready to go back to work right now.

"No. I won't let you go just now," he said. "You look like you're dead, and besides, don't worry, I saved your life once. I won't let anything happen to you now." With that, I thanked him for saving me and left.

Back at my old barracks, the bunk I had used wasn't occupied, so for the next two days I did nothing but loaf around. At midmorning on the third day, a policeman came to the barracks and read a list of six names. I was one of them so I went outside with the other five.

"You are going to work," he said. As we started walking to the factory, I looked at the other men. They didn't look too good to me. They could hardly walk and were very thin. They looked sick. I wondered why they didn't take me to work with everyone else the first thing in the morning.

We got to the factory and the Jewish policeman told us to wait outside while he went into the office. Soon the German boss who replaced Laidik came out with the policeman. He looked us over and told us we were all going to Palestine, as he pointed his finger at the sky. I'd heard him use that expression before, during selection. He meant we were going to die. Then, he went back into his office.

The policeman took us back to camp and told us to go back to the barracks. This didn't sound good to me. What usually happened was that when there were enough people like us, rejects, the Ukrainians would take us into the forest. I didn't understand. I came out alive from the typhoid fever, the German commandant spared me, I was better now and could work, but now they don't want me. They will kill me anyhow. I seemed to be facing death every minute I was here. Sometimes I envied the dead. I was getting tired, so tired of living like this. I was just a kid, but I felt like an old man. I was tired of being scared, hungry, and dirty, living day to day not knowing if I would live to see tomorrow.

Two days went by and nothing happened. I felt I was living on borrowed time. The Germans weren't going to feed us for nothing, they weren't that benevolent. On the third day, a policeman entered the barracks and made an announcement:

"All the names I call will report to the police headquarters immediately." He called my name, and when I got there, there were many other people. We lined up outside and each person went in separately.

When it was my turn, I pushed in the door to the commandant's room and saw five policemen sitting around the desk. One of them was my brother's friend, the one who was going to help me. When he saw me, he turned his head away. The assistant Jewish chief of police asked me my name and I told him. He looked at the other policemen; they nodded their heads so he told me that tomorrow morning I would be transferred to camp A to work.

"Take all of your possessions with you," I was told. I thought, all what possessions? My container for soup? That was all I had in this whole stinking world. Outside, I looked over the people who were still lined up to go inside. No, we weren't going to camp A. They were just telling us that. They would take us to camp C, to the forest. That's where they were going to take us, out to the forest to kill us. They were telling us camp A because they didn't want a panic. Once again, I resigned myself to my fate.

The next morning the Jewish policeman called everyone outside to line up. Two Ukrainians waited by the camp gate. They marched us out. It was slow going; some people had to be helped by others because they cold hardly walk. I couldn't help thinking that I wasn't sorry to leave this hellhole and the rest of this lousy world. I had no family, no friends, I was all alone, so who cared. Not me, anymore.

To my surprise, the Ukrainians took us to camp A. So, I was wrong again. Well, well. The Jewish policemen weren't lying after all. My surprise didn't last long. When we got there, a group of people were waiting. They joined us and we headed back on the road to camp C. I wasn't wrong after all. The group from camp A didn't look any better than we did. It was a long walk, and by the time we arrived at factory C, it was getting dark. Nobody talked. Everyone must have been deep in their own thoughts like me. I was thinking about how easy it was for us be led, just like sheep to slaughter.

CHAPTER XII

The Ukrainian guard opened the gate to the factory. There must have been a hundred of us. Our guard stopped us just inside the gate. About a half-dozen Ukrainians joined the original guards and told us to line up. Men in white coats came out of a building and walked over to where we were standing. I thought they were German bosses and that they were going to select us for work. Some men were told to step out. One of the men in a white jacket with a very kind face and smile told me:

"Come out boy." I stepped out. Then the Ukrainian guard selected nineteen others. The rest were led away. The guard who picked me told me to report in the morning to Department Six. Then a Jewish policeman came over and led our small group away. After a long walk, we arrived at the camp where we were assigned to various barracks. Camp C was twice as large as camp B. I felt funny there, out of place, lost.

It was strange to see all the activity. Two streets ran between rows of barracks, and a big square was situated on the side of the camp, near the gate. Each barracks was numbered. There was such a contrast between the people there. Some were well dressed and healthy, while others walked around looking like they were dead, but just too tired to lie down. I found out later that they were called the 'Walking Dead.' They had the look of skeletons, no meaty flesh, just skin covering the bones, their minds gone. They wandered around aimlessly until, finally, one day they just lay down and that was the end. It was pitiful to watch them. It was a mystery to me, even to this day, years later, how they got that way.

For the first time, I noticed people whose skin was deep yellow in color. Later, I found out these were the people working in a plant that manufactured land mines. The material they used was yellow and penetrated their skin. Their work was considered very dangerous. They put yellow powder in forms, which were pressed into hard cubes. The cubes then went into steel containers, with the end result being powerful explosives.

Many times when the form was not in perfect position in the press, there would be an explosion, killing whomever was working around it. When the explosions occurred, the Germans called it sabotage, and the person that operated the press (if he lived through the explosion) was taken into the forest and shot.

At night, I could see dead bodies piled alongside the barracks. They were the people who had died during the day or night. If bodies were in the way, they were merely piled up outside, 'out of the way.' Each day a man came by, pushing a handcart, taking the bodies to an area behind the hospital, situated in the corner of the camp. He would dump them there and once a week, a truck transported the bodies into the forest.

I was assigned to barracks number ten. I found an empty bunk, crawled in and fell asleep.

In the morning, I lined up with the group that was to work in Department Six. After roll call, we arrived at a big long building where they manufactured 100-pound artillery shells. The building was divided into three rooms. Empty steel casings were housed in a small room at one end of the building, where they were delivered. Next to that room was a very large boiler. Men dumped yellow powder into it, added water, and boiled the mixture. Meanwhile, the shells were placed on conveyor rollers and, as they moved along, were filled with the mixture through a spigot in the bottom of the boiler. The mixture was then boiled again.

The shells were placed on conveyor rollers that moved along beneath the boiler. A spigot on the bottom of the boiler filled the shell casings with the hot liquid. The women workers handled the next steps of the manufacturing process. As the conveyor led to another room, each filled shell had to be tamped down with a steel rod, mixing the hot liquid as it cooled into a hard pack. Women stood on both sides of the rolling conveyor to keep up with the shells speeding along the line. Girls at the end of the assembly line added plastic caps to the shells. Warheads were not installed here.

In the next room there was a long low table where the women scrubbed the shells with long steel brushes. Farther down the table, the shells were cleaned with rags dipped in gasoline. In front of the table, with a man on each side, the shells were laid downward, where the women finished cleaning them.

At the other end of the table, two men took the shells off and stacked them on a cart that sat on rails and went through the whole factory, like train tracks. Then other men transported the finished shells to a warehouse where they were unloaded and stacked. In some places, the stacks reached all the way to the ceiling. Every so often, a train came right up to the siding, close to the factory while more men loaded the shells onto the train.

When I got to the factory the first thing in the morning, a Polish foreman put me at the table with another man, to lift the shells onto it. At first it wasn't too bad, but as the day progressed, it got harder and harder for me to lift the heavy shells. By evening I didn't know if I had the strength to lift my container of soup. I knew that if I worked in that spot for any length of time, it would kill me.

But whom could I complain to? I talked to the Jewish foreman, but he told me he couldn't do anything about it. There was no use to talk to the Polish policeman; he's the one who put me there in the first place. He might even report me to the Germans and that would be the end for me. So, I plugged along for a week. The next week I went on the night shift. After working a couple of hours on that first night, a young German walked through the department. He was short and stocky, wore the uniform of a sergeant of the regular army. On one hand, he wore a leather glove. He must have lost his hand during the war, but was still working for the war effort.

I didn't see him standing there watching me since my back was toward him. He must have been standing there for quite some time. A man I was working with saw him and started working faster. I took the hint, lifting the shells onto the table faster than I ever had before. I could feel someone was staring at my back as I tried to work even a little faster. Then the German call out, "Hey, you. Come over here." My partner told me that the German wanted me. I turned to face him.

"Come here," he repeated. I walked over to him, uncertainly. "What's your name?" he asked.

"Henry," I told him.

"No, Henry is not a Jewish name," he retorted. "Your name is Joseph."

"Yes sir," I said. He could call me anything he liked. After all, he was one of my masters. I wondered what he wanted from me. Wasn't I working fast enough for his liking? Then he asked me if I had a container for soup, which confused me.

"Yes, I have," I answered.

"Where is it?" He wanted to know. I pointed to the window ledge.

"Come with me," he said and started walking very briskly as I followed, although I could hardly keep up with him. Once outside the building, he started trotting.

"Come run, Joseph. It's good for you." So I ran along side of him, trying to keep up. I was so confused! Was this man crazy or something? We ran all the way to the kitchen.

The kitchen smelled good; soup for the night shift was cooking in two huge boilers. As the aroma filtered through my nostrils, I realized how hungry I was. The German told the Polish cook to fill my container with soup. Without a question, the cook did as he was told. The German turned to me.

"That will fatten you up. Let's go back," he said.

Back at the factory, he summoned the foreman and told him to put an older man in my spot to lift shells onto the table. I thanked him.

"Go ahead and sit down," he replied and walked away. I was shocked, but very happy. Not only did I have a full container of soup, (not having had so much soup at one time since I'd been in the camps, but now I had an easy job, too). I couldn't help thinking what a nice man this German was – a Nazi with a heart. It was hard to believe. I soon found out about him. He was an overseer in Department Fifty-One, which manufactured twelve-pound artillery shells that were being equipped with warheads, and each one was packed in wooden crates. One had to be very careful with those shells or they might blow up.

One day a Polish worker was packing the shells and put a finished shell into the crate. When it didn't fit, he started to pound the shell on the table and it blew up. Fifty people around the area were blown to bits. It was said that the Pole was drunk at the time.

I was told that the German soldier who liked me was a real killer. He constantly picked on the Jews in his department for no reason at all. And when he beat them, he did such a thorough job that they either died right there in the factory, or they never came back to work again.

I tried to figure him out. Apparently, I was his Jew, but he hated the rest. Every so often he came in and handed me something wrapped in paper, usually bread, but sometimes a real meat and cheese sandwich. He never said much, just handed me what he had and left. I heard all the stories about him and found it difficult to believe it was the same man that they were all talking about.

Once, during lunchtime, our Jewish policeman was dishing out our soup and, for one reason or another, he was in a bad mood. He spilled the soup and screamed at everyone. When it was my turn, I held my container out very carefully so he wouldn't spill this very precious liquid. He deliberately spilled the soup on my hands. It was very hot and I dropped the container. At that, the policeman started screaming about what a clumsy clod I was and smacked me in the face as he told me that I wasn't getting any soup. I picked up the container, which had only a few drops of soup left in it, and moved away from the line.

Unbeknown to me, my German friend had observed everything that went on. He called me over and asked if my hands were all right. I said they were, even though they were red and burning where the soup had spilled. He told me to wait, then screamed at the Jewish policeman to come over. The policeman rushed over and snapped to attention. The German slapped him in the face with his good hand with such force that the policeman's hat flew off his head.

"You touch this boy again, and I'll kill you," shouted the German.

"Yes sir!"

"Now go and give him his soup."

"Yes sir!"

The German motioned for me to follow the policeman very carefully. I did, and I could see all five finger marks on his face where the German had slapped him, and I worried that he would do it to me, later. But I didn't have to worry. Since that incident, the policeman became a good friend of mine and gave me extra soup. He always talked to me with respect after that.

Even though this camp was more notorious than camp B, life became more bearable for me. I thought how ironic this whole situation was. They brought me here to die, but instead I lived better here than I did in camp B.

We heard all kinds of rumors about the war, which the Germans were losing in Russia. Then one day we heard that Hitler was dead, killed by his own general. Everyone was happy, but not for long. The next day we heard another story that an attempt was made on his life, but didn't succeed. He was alive and kicking! Too bad, because we felt that if Hitler was dead, the war would end, and all of the Jews would be freed. No such luck!

July 20, 1944 People were dying left and right as executions in camp increased. There was something new going on. Every few days, convoys of trucks went by the factory on their way into the forest. We found out there were people in the trucks. Small steel boxes were mounted on top of the trucks. News came through the underground movement that those trucks carried Polish dissidents. The boxes on top of the trucks contained cyanide gas, which was automatically released by the driver. The prisoners were dead before they reached their destination, the forest. The Germans had erected a new building with a chimney in the forest. Eventually, we found out it was a crematorium for those bodies.

When the wind blew toward the factory after that, the stench was awful. The Germans began holding executions on Sundays. They were probably doing that because on Sunday, everyone was at home and they were forced to watch.

One Sunday, two Germans, one in a SS uniform and the other in a leather coat and hat, brought over a young man in chains. The Jewish police chased everyone out into the square. The two Germans and the young Jewish man stood in the middle of the square. The man, obviously, had been beaten. The SS man was holding the end of the long chain, which was wrapped around the man's neck, his hands and his waist. He stood with his head down, ready to die. How pitiful he looked! He apparently was resigned to his fate. Then, the commandant of the camp reported to the Germans that everyone was present. The German in the leather coat pulled out a revolver from under his coat, put it to the man's temple and pulled the trigger. The shot rang out and the man fell to the ground.

"Any of you other pigs want to escape?" the German officer yelled. After a short wait (as if someone was going to answer), he turned without further words and walked out of the camp.

I began thinking as I looked around. There were about eight hundred of us and only two Germans, yet they can do with us as they please. I wondered if anyone here had feelings for the young man who just lost his life. I doubted that they did. I do, but who am I? With all emotions having been drained from bodies, I think that the only thing they feel is the inconvenience of having been chased out to stand in the square until it was over, on their day of rest.

The only reason that we got a day of rest was because they hadn't figured out any other way to make the shift change from nights to days and days to nights. Here, each person was for him or her self. I concluded, that's the way it had to be since no one else really cared.

Shortly thereafter, the men who worked with bodies picked up the dead man, scooping him up into the pushcart. They carried him off and dumped him behind the hospital barracks.

My mind wandered again. Why did this man try to escape? Didn't he know there was no place to go where he would be safe? Didn't he know the Polish people were not the friends of the Jews? Didn't he know that the Germans offered five pounds of sugar to any Pole who had information of the whereabouts of any Jew? Well, I guess that for some Jews, anything was better than this rotten place, even death.

Two weeks after the young man was shot, we were all called out to the square for another execution. This time eight men were to be hung for sabotage. They had cut and stolen the rubber hoses that connected railroad boxcars and sold them to a Polish man who used rubber to fix the soles of shoes. One evening, the Polish man was stopped at the gate on his way home and searched. The Germans found the rubber pieces on him and he instantly incriminated one of the Jewish men who had sold it to him. The Gestapo picked up the Jewish man and after they worked him over, he named the other seven who were involved and they all ended up confessing. The Gestapo had ways to make people talk.

The eight men were brought from Gestapo headquarters in town and put in a small room guarded by Jewish policemen. The other policemen chased everyone into the square. The men would be hung from two big trees growing to the side of the square. Several Germans were gathered in the middle of the square: the German commandant, the guards, a few SS men, the Gestapo men in their leather coats, a few bosses from the factory and three German women, (their wives, I suppose). They stood in a group, joking and laughing, like people did at some of the parties we had back home in Plock.

The Jewish policemen brought the eight saboteurs outside. Two of them were dragged, as if they couldn't walk. All of them appeared to be in a daze, heads hung down and not seeming to know where they were. Among them was a young boy no more than sixteen. Not far from where I was standing, an older man was looking toward the group and crying. Someone next to me said that he was the father of the young boy about to be hung.

The hanging was to be done by a Jewish man who, from what I understood, had done this sort of thing before. The Germans didn't do dirty jobs like that. They just enjoyed watching. The men who were helping with the executions tied the prisoners' hands behind their backs and one by one; a noose was placed around their necks and tightened. One by one, the ropes were thrown across the limb of the tree. Two of the helpers pulled hard on the rope until each man's body was about two feet off the ground, then fastened the loose end around the trunk of the tree. There were four men on one tree, four men on the other. Oh, how the prisoners were suffering. Their bodies twitched and jerked until finally they were still.

Through his tears, the father of the young boy recited a Jewish prayer for the dead. I felt so sorry for him. I knew how he mush have felt, seeing his own son being hung right before his eyes.

The German commandant ordered the bodies to be left hanging for the rest of the day and night and the Germans left, talking joyfully. I ran to a corner and vomited. The next morning the bodies were still hanging there, swaying gently in the breeze. For a long time I couldn't forget that sight. Would this nightmare ever end? Would I get out of here alive? I was not very optimistic about it. In the end, they would kill us all.

There were no more transports. Apparently, there weren't any Jews left in Poland; the Germans must have murdered the ones who were left in their homes. Were there any more concentration camps like this in Poland? For that matter, in Europe? Nobody here knew. We worked, ate and slept and tried to stay alive.

A month had gone by since the hangings. All was normal until one evening after work. Everyone was chased out of the barracks and into the square, where the German commandant waited with the Jewish commandant. Once everyone was outside, the German told us that the camp was going to be evacuated starting the next night. After work that day, everyone was to report to the square and be registered by him. He added that the weak people would travel by train, the strong ones by foot. With that we were dismissed.

Back in the barracks, people tried to evaluate the situation. Where were they taking us? It couldn't be very far if some of us are going on foot. Something was wrong. Since when have the Germans been so benevolent that they would transport the weak by train?

I didn't trust the Germans. They had always lied to the Jews, and this time wasn't going to be any different. All night the discussion went on in the barracks, but no one came up with a logical answer. The only thing we all agreed on was to wait and see.

The next day in the factory, I heard news from the Poles that the Russians were now in Poland and chasing the Germans back and that they should be in this area within days. I hoped so, but I had a feeling that the Russians might not be here in time to liberate our camp. Either the Germans would kill us all, or evacuate us right in front of the Russians' noses.

That night, everyone in camp lined up in the square. The

German commandant was seated behind a desk with a list of our names in front of him. As we approached him, we told him our names. He looked at each person and made a mark on one list or the other. When I told him my name and he looked at me while making his mark, I tried to read his eyes. Where was he putting me? But his eyes were cold and without expression. Was I considered one of the weak ones?

Two days went by. Stories about the Russian advancement were spreading throughout the camp. Would they get here in time? Tension grew among the people. Some lay on the ground in the square to listen. By doing that, some said they could hear artillery fire. All of a sudden, everyone was an expert on the war, claiming to know how far we were from the front lines. Well, I should know, too, so I lay down on the grass with my ear to the ground. Sure enough! I heard a noise like explosions, but it also sounded like they were far away.

Tomorrow was the day the night shift wouldn't work in the evening, which meant one thing! I couldn't sleep all night, trying to figure out what the Germans had in store for us next. Would they kill us? No, if they had that in mind, why did the commandant make a list? Maybe that was a diversion to avoid panic. The Germans were good at that. Maybe they would only kill the weak ones. After all, they still needed slaves to work somewhere else. I only wished I knew which list I was on. But even if I knew, what could I do? Escape? To where? If I got caught, I would know for sure what my fate was.

Early the next morning the Jewish policeman chased everyone out into the square and told us to take our belongings. (Yes, I was going to take all my belongings with me – my soup container.)

The German commandant stood in the middle of the square with the list in his hand. There were a few trucks waiting outside the camp gate, and two Ukrainian guards stood next to them. Why so many guards? The commandant addressed the assembly.

"The names I will call, come forward. You will go on the train," he announced. He started calling names and those people whose names were called stepped forward. There were about twenty of them. Then, five Ukrainians took them to the trucks and loaded them on board like bales of hay.

As they left, the commandant called more names. I noticed that some of the names he called were not answered and he didn't wait for them to come forward. He just kept calling more names. I had been in the camp long enough to know that something wasn't right. They were in too big off a hurry. Of the names on the list, only five people came forward and were picked up by the Ukrainians. I thought the people who were picked did not look good. My assumption was that the people who were picked up would be going only as far as the forest, and that a lot of people weren't coming forward when called, proved to me that they had the same idea I did. He called my name and I froze on the spot. The commandant continued to call out names. Some people were coming forward and were scooped up by the guards and put into the trucks. I felt nothing but panic. They wouldn't stop here. I told myself that I must hide. But where? There was a crawl space under the barracks, but they would look there. They would look inside them, too. Where could I hide? I started moving backwards until I found myself standing next to one of the barracks. That was it! The hospital barracks had the pile of dead bodies in the back. No one would look for me there.

I made my move onto the road between the two rows of barracks, moving fast. Thank God, there was still enough confusion in camp so they didn't see me. The Jewish police were still chasing people out of their barracks and it was pandemonium around me. I didn't see the policeman until I ran into him.

"Where do you think you're going?" he demanded.

"To get my things," I answered shaking.

"Well, be quick about it!" he said and let me go. That was a close call. The hospital barracks was quiet. I looked around to see if I was being watched. Then I dashed behind the barracks.

There it was, the big pile of dead bodies. Very carefully, I lay down next to the corpses trying to look like I belonged there. Someone had stripped the bodies of their clothing. I lay very still, trying to blend in and afraid to move, almost afraid to breathe. I was so horrified I was shivering, but slowly I calmed down until I was motionless. I kept telling myself that they were all dead and couldn't hurt me, like they were all rag dolls that someone had tossed away after playing with them.

I fought with myself. These had been living people. Some might even have been alive this morning. Yes, but my life depended on lying here, I reminded myself. The smell was horrible. I couldn't stand it. I'm going to be sick! My thoughts raged, but I stayed. I had been lying there for quite a long time. No, maybe half an hour, but it seemed like a long time.

Then I heard footsteps. My heart stopped. A truck pulled up and I heard a voice say, "Okay, let's get it over with." They started dragging people out from the barracks and I heard faint cries. I'd better lie down on top of the pile in case they look here, too. So I did.

Oh, God! Who was this? Whose face was my face touching? Who was this person when he was alive? He must have had a name. If I didn't go mad this moment, my nerves were stronger than I thought. I could still hear voices in the barracks. It seemed like I had been here forever. Would they ever leave? I almost felt like getting up and telling them to take me. No! Lie down. They will leave soon.

Was I thinking these thoughts, or was I talking out loud? I couldn't tell anymore. Dear God, what else must I do to stay alive? Now, now! Stop feeling sorry for yourself. Remember, where there is life, there is hope. You are still alive. These poor souls under you are dead. You are better off than they are. You are alive! Maybe, maybe, they are better off. They have no more worries. They aren't scared or hungry any more. They don't have to fight for this stinking existence any more.

Finally, I heard the trucks leaving. Then there were footsteps, coming around the back of the barracks. There were two of them.

"What are you looking for?" one asked the other. "There's nothing but stiffs."

"Yes, I guess you're right. Come on, let's go." They left. They were both Jewish policemen. I wondered if they would hand me over to the Germans if they found me here. Yes, they would. Sometimes I think they were no better than the Germans.

Things had been quiet for a while, so I climbed down from the pile and lay down at the edge. They weren't all gone yet. I could hear screaming coming from the square, then shots and more screams. I felt I should try to escape. It would be easy. I was about five feet from the barbed wire fence, and beyond the fence was the thick forest. If what they said about the Russians being just around the corner was true, then I could wait in the forest until they came. But what if the Russians were still far away? I might starve to death. I wouldn't dare go to town. What should I do?

The screams coming from the square were continuous now, and so was the shooting. Yes, I should jump over the fence and be free. It sounded like they were shooting everyone who was left in camp. It would take no time at all and I would be discovered.

I crouched down, ready to run for the fence when I spotted a Ukrainian guard coming down the path outside the fence. I dropped to the ground. I inched my way back to the pile of bodies and played dead again. The guard was only a few feet away. I held my breath. Now he was almost on top of me. He stopped at the corner, took his rifle off his shoulder and propped it against the fence, and then he pulled out a pack of cigarettes from his breast pocket and lit one. If I breathed, would he hear me? Would he see my body move from the intake of air? I better not breathe.

He finished his cigarette and stubbed it out on the ground, but he didn't leave; instead, he leaned against the fence. I thought he was going to take a nap. I was so wrapped up in this latest horror that the dead bodies didn't bother me any more. They might as well be rag dolls! That guard spoiled my plan. He stood with his arms around his chest, his back against the fence; he was sleeping. I didn't dare go to the fence now. He might wake up, and that would be certain death for me. The noise from the square continued: screams, shots, then more screams and more shooting. Would it ever end?

It must have been late in the afternoon because the sun was slowly going down. Finally, the guard woke up. He slung his rifle over his shoulder and walked away. I breathed easier now. The sun was setting and the square activities were quieting down. I left my hiding place and went to the corner of the barracks to look around. There were people walking around in the distance. I made my way to my own barracks. I didn't realize that a Jewish policeman was watching me. He was standing next to the hospital.

"What have you been doing there?" he asked. I had to think fast. I told him I was saying goodbye to my friend.

"Get out of here, you wise guy," he said. And I moved away fast.

As I walked to the barracks, I noticed an unusually small number of people walking around camp. Where was everyone? When I arrived at my barracks, I found it half empty, not like the usual Sunday when both shifts were home and one could hardly move about.

I found the man who slept next to me. He told me what had happened during the day. It seemed that less and less people showed themselves when the commandant read the list of names. So, finally, he gave up altogether. Reinforcements were called and soon a truck full of SS men arrived. They surrounded the square so no one could get out. The SS men searched every inch of the camp and whoever they found was brought to the commandant. They did a good job. They even found one man hiding under the floorboards beneath the toilet.

He also said that they were herding everyone to one side of the camp square. Then, each person had to walk down to where the commandant was standing. Anyone who refused to go was shot on the spot. A mother and her daughter were standing together. One guard tried to take the mother, and the daughter wouldn't let her go, so the guard shot both of them on the spot. It seemed like half of the people in the camp were gone.

That night was very traumatic for everyone. We were talking about the people we knew who were gone. I felt that life here was so cheap, one minute you are alive and the next you are dead. It was hard to fall asleep that night.

CHAPTER XIII

The morning brought us screams from the Jewish policeman to come to the camp square again where the Ukrainian guards were waiting for us. The lived us up and counted every body. They opened the gates and we started marching towards the railroad station in town. They crowded us like sardines into boxcars. The fear of the unknown creeps into my mind. Where are they taking us? Where are we going?

The train ride from Skarzyskko Kamienna took a day and a half. We had been packed into the boxcars, suffering from hunger. Tempers were very short. Many times fights would start among the men, at the slightest provocation. In spite of that, each of us arrived in one piece.

When the journey finally ended, we found ourselves at the doors of a factory in the suburb of Chestochowa. The town was known as the place where a miracle occurred, a vision of the Black Madonna appeared and the Polish Catholics erected a shrine in commemoration of the event. Poles from all over the country had made pilgrimages there.
The factory we would be working in manufactured munitions. There was a large steel mill about five miles from there.

The Ukrainian guards started screaming at everyone to get off the train. A huge square surrounded the factory buildings. People were mingling. I began looking for anyone I knew from camp B. I found a few who told me the fate of people at camp B was the same as those from camp C.

The Jewish policemen from this camp came into the square and called for every man from camp C to line up on one side. They counted heads and informed us that we were going to work in the steel mill. I was not very happy when I heard that news. They were taking only men from camp C because they knew the men were used to heavy work, and I could imagine that the work at the steel mill would be very heavy.

On the way to the mill, I recognized two men who weren't from C, but from camp B. One was a Jewish policeman and the other (no surprise to me), was the former Jewish police chief, Jarmolf. They were coming with us because they knew no one would know them here. Little did they know that I was here, and that I recognized them both.

The camp was small, only a half dozen barracks. The people in this camp looked much better than us, better dressed and much healthier looking. I found out they were taken from the town of Chestochowa. They even had their own bedding that they were allowed to bring from home. I hadn't seen bedding like this in a long time.

I also met two brothers from my hometown, Plock. They were older than I, but still young men. They told me that a small group of people from Plock was brought here to Chestochowa and that, eventually, the Germans liquidated the Jews from the town and some of the young people were taken to the two camps.

We were assigned to different barracks. There was only one Jewish commandant and two policemen and they seemed to be decent people. I didn't see anyone being beaten or even screamed at. How different it was from the camp where Jarmolf was in charge. He and the policemen who came here with him changed their names so as not to be recognized. Yes, this was much different than camp B.

The first night I went from one barracks to another until I found the two of them. Although they were staying in the same barracks, they avoided each other so no one would know who or what they were. I didn't know why the policeman didn't want to be recognized; he wasn't quite as bad as some of the others and certainly nothing like Jarmolf.

The barracks was very crowded and I had to push my way to where Jarmolf sat on an upper bunk, his legs dangling. I stood in front of him, but he didn't notice me. He was talking to a man next to him. When I tapped his shoes, he looked down at me.

"Remember me?" I asked. His face became a mask of disbelief and terror. I smiled at him. With his eyes as big as saucers, he stared at me but didn't say a word. I said no more to him either. I just turned around and walked out of the barracks.

I decided that I was going to do that every night and worry him to death. Let him live in terror every minute of every day, not knowing if or when I would squeal on him. I learned fast.

The next day, the Jewish commandant assigned us our work. He chose two other young boys and me to work at the big oven and told us not to worry, the work was not hard. They needed someone to keep the generator room warm and it would be our job to fill the potbellied stove with coal and make sure the fire didn't go out. We were assigned to the department that had a middle-aged foreman who seemed to be a very nice man.

The mill was a short distance from the camp. When we got there, the foreman showed us the room that we were to keep warm. It was nice and cozy there. I felt I was going to like this! We worked the same schedule as we had before, one week days and one week nights. Since there were three of us, we could take turns look-ing after the fire and do other things. I explored the factory. There were two departments there. One contained the big oven and the other produced wire. The big oven was about three stories high. At the top the raw materials, such as iron ore, scrap metal and coke, were loaded. The finished cast iron came out the bottom.

A big room adjacent to the oven had sand forms, which had to be watered all the time to keep the sand in shape. Once a day the oven was opened and the red-hot liquid iron was poured into the sand forms and left there until it cooled off. The pouring of the hot iron was a very dangerous operation because if there was one drop of water left in the sand forms when it was poured, it would explode on contact in the form of splashes. The burn from the splashes was so bad a few people had died.

When the iron cooled, men with big hammers broke the bars. It was a three-man operation. The hammer had a rope attached to it on each side. One man held the handle and on each side another man held the rope. All these picked up the hammer at the same time and smashed it on the groove between the iron bars to separate them It was very hard work. Some Polish men worked here, but, mostly, the Jewish men did the really hard work.

The next morning when the iron bars were cold, other men picked them up and loaded them on to carts that were sitting on rails to be hauled to the yard outside and stacked. The work in this department was so tough; I felt that if I worked there, I wouldn't last very long.

In the other department where wire was made, there was a smaller oven. When the hot steel was poured out, it went into steel forms of another kind and set very quickly. The hot steel was fed into rollers and a press, and came out in a block. A man was stationed on each side of the machine to grab this block and guide it into another press. At the other end of this last press, there was a man with a long device that guided the thin wire around a spool. This work was also very dangerous. I heard about men who weren't paying attention to the wire coming out of the final press and were killed when the wire went through their bodies. I wouldn't like working there either. Even though it was very hot in there, the men had to wear heavy shirts because of the hot slivers of steel flying aimlessly through the air.

Railroad tracks filled the large yard outside the factory, making it easier for transporting the finished product to wherever they wanted. The Polish workers in the factory were a nice bunch of men who worked hard and bothered no one, which was why I could go all over the factory and explore with no limitations. I did still have to watch out for the Ukrainian guards. They seemed to be almost invisible except for the one at the gate of the camp.

Every evening there was a call by one of the Jewish policemen for anyone who wanted to take a shower. That was a luxury we hadn't had for years.

My foreman stayed in the same barracks as the ex-chief of police and the ex-policeman from camp B. He distributed the soup and portion of bread. Every night, we went to his barracks to get our portions. I made it a point to continue my visits to the ex-chief Jarmolf. I just stood there in front of him and smiled, then walked away without saying a word. I really did worry him. The ex-policeman recognized me also, but he avoided me as much as possible. I really had nothing against him, but the chief was another matter. It would be so easy to finger him and his life would be worth nothing. But I wouldn't do that. I'd rather worry him to death, just like I was doing.

One evening, one of the brothers from Plock asked me to come with him to his barracks, because some people wanted to talk to me. When I obliged, I found a bunch of young men sitting around a table in a corner of the room. One of them spoke up. He told me that he knew I was in camp B in Skarzysko. I told him that he was right. He went on to say that they knew there was a Jewish police chief from camp B in this camp now.

"We want you to tell us who he is," he said.

"I don't know anyone here from camp B," I answered. He then became quite upset with me and accused me of lying.

"Just point him out to me and we will kill him. You know he was a bastard, beating people and sending the rest to death."

"Yes, I remember him, but he isn't here." They were losing patience with me. One of them grabbed me and put his fist in front of my nose.

"Look, if you don't talk, you're going to get a beating," he threatened.

"Go ahead! You can beat me all you want, but how can I tell you anything when I don't see the man here?"

Finally, they let me go. Then, I thought to myself: Jarmolf deserves to die, but I will not be the one responsible for his death. I won't have what they do to him on my conscience. Let someone else point the finger, not me. I would just continue doing what I was doing to him: worry him to death.

The very next night the boys grabbed the ex-policeman, took him into their barracks and beat him, thinking he was the ex-chief. He said nothing other than to deny he was the chief they were looking for. They promised him another beating each night until he admitted he was the police chief.

Right after work the next evening, the ex-policeman came into my barracks looking for me. He told me about the beating he had gotten the night before and pleaded with me to tell the boys that he wasn't the one they were looking for.

"Then, you want me to tell them who the commandant is?" I said. "Why don't you tell them who he is?"

"They won't believe me no matter what I tell them, and they promised to kill me. Please, I beg you to tell them who it is," he pleaded.

"No," I said rather sternly. "I won't tell them who he is. However, I don't know why I should help you, but I will. I'll go right now and tell them you are not the chief. By the way, why did you come here?"

"Well, you know I wasn't a bad guy at camp B, but we were talking among ourselves before we left and decided, if possible, we would go where no one knows us. I saw the opportunity here and that's why I came here."

"That makes sense. As for Jarmolf, he will still get what is coming to him." I went over to the other barracks and told one of the brothers that I knew the man they had beaten the night before, and would probably end up killing, was not the police chief.

"By the way," I asked, "what makes you think the police chief is here?" He answered that they were in contact with the other camp in town and were told by someone there that Jarmolf was here. He was seen on the train coming here, then disappeared, so they assumed he was here.

"Well," I told them very convincingly, "maybe he escaped. He is not in this camp. I don't know, but he isn't in this camp." I think they believed my story. At least, the policeman wasn't bothered anymore. I knew I might get myself in a heap of trouble if they found out who the chief really was and that he was here in this camp. At least, my conscience was clear and I wasn't an informer.

I continued my little game. Every night I went into the other barracks and smiled at Jarmolf. My cynical smile was driving him crazy. I wondered if he knew what was going on, if he knew they were looking for him. One thing I did know for sure, he was fully aware that his life was in my hands. Knowing that he knows that gives me a great feeling. I would continue this forever or at least until...whatever.

Winter was coming again and I wasn't looking forward to it. One week while I was on the night shift, one of my co-workers came in and told me that a train had arrived not long ago and that one car was loaded with potatoes and no one was guarding it.

I asked one of the boys I worked with to go with me to get some potatoes. We found an old bucket and set off to find the boxcar. It was dark and hard to see. When we found the boxcar, I told the boy to stand guard while I climbed to the top of it.

"If you see anyone coming, whistle," I said. I filled the bucket with potatoes and got ready to hand it down to the other boy, but I couldn't see him. I strained my eyes searching, then called his name as quietly as I could, but he didn't answer. He must have gotten cold feet and took off on me. Well, who needed him anyway? I could do it myself. I put one leg over the side and held the bucket in one hand while I used the other to inch my way down. It was tricky, trying to get off without falling, or most importantly, without spilling any of the precious potatoes. Suddenly, a German shepherd let out a mean growl and leaped at me. As fast as I could, I scratched my way back up to the top of the boxcar while the dog barked viciously and leaped up to bite me. A Ukrainian guard stood near the dog, motioning to me with his finger to come down. I shook my head no.

The guard then told me to come down. I hesitated, looking into the jaws of the dog. If I came down, the dog might tear me to pieces, if the guard let him. These dogs were trained killers. Then the guard took his rifle from his shoulder and pointed it at me.

"Come down," he ordered, "and bring the potatoes with you." I had no choice so, with my back to the dog, I started down. I had to jump the last few feet and the potatoes scattered. I fell to the ground as well. The dog tried to bite my head, so I covered it with my arms, but the dog started on my arms, tearing my sleeves. I felt his teeth on my skin.

The guard called off the dog. The dog obeyed immediately. He told me to pick up the potatoes and put them back in the bucket. I obeyed. He leashed the dog and told me to walk in front of him. As I walked ahead, he nudged me with the rifle periodically. He was taking me to headquarters, which meant that I had a good beating coming.

Before we got to our destination, the handle of the bucket broke, spilling the potatoes again. He made me pick them up as the dog kept nipping at my legs. He didn't break the skin, but the teeth were sharp.

When we arrived outside the headquarters, the guard told me to leave the bucket there. Indoors, there were three other Ukrainians sitting around smoking cigarettes and talking. He told the dog to sit in the corner of the room. The dog obeyed, but was prepared to leap at me at the slightest command. The guard told the others that he had caught me stealing potatoes. They all stood up, grabbed their clubs and told me to bend over.

"We'll give him fifty lashes," said one.

"No, he's a young kid. Twenty will be enough," another one said.

"Okay, twenty-five it is. Start counting." I did. The first blow went through me like an electric shock. I'd better not make a mistake in counting, or goof off. I knew better from the last time. Soon I didn't feel much of the pain. "Twenty-four – twenty-five." Not a whimper from me all through the beating. They told me to get up.

"Tough kid, aren't you," one of them said. They told me to get out and go back to work. Uncertain of their next move, I slowly started toward the door with one eye on the guards and one on the dog. The dog sat in the corner quivering, as if any minute he would leap at me and tear my skin off. To my surprise, the door was not locked. I closed it behind me and noticed the bucket of potatoes. So that the beating would not be in vain, I grabbed some of them, put them in my pockets and started running. My body hurt and burned, but I ran until I got to the factory, where I saw the boy who was supposed to help me. He looked nervous. When I asked him what happened, he said he got scared when he saw the guard with the dog and ran away. I thanked him for his loyalty. I showed him my potatoes.

Back at the barracks, it seemed that the whole camp knew what happened to me. A short time later, one of the Jewish policemen came in and told me to come along because the camp commandant wanted to see me. When I got to the commandant's office, he really gave me a tongue-lashing.

"What the hell do you think you were doing? Don't you know that he could have killed you? There has never been a death in this camp yet, and I am here to see to it that it doesn't happen." I apologized to him and promised never to do it again. He then asked if I was hurt.

"Just a little, but I'm all right," I said.

"I want you to go to the dispensary," he demanded, "and have the doctor look at your wounds." I promised to do that immediately. On the way to the doctor, I couldn't help thinking what a nice man the commandant was. I didn't think there were any Jews left who had concern for anyone but themselves. When I went in to see the doctor, I wondered what he could do for me. He told me to take off my pants, then he looked at my backside, listened to my back and said it looked nasty, but I would be all right. I figured he didn't have any medicine to use on me.

Two weeks after I got caught trying to steal potatoes, another boy tried the same thing in broad daylight. He worked the same job as I did, but on different shifts. A guard surprised him by shouting at him to stop, but the boy started running. The guard shot him in the back and killed him.

The commandant went to retrieve the body. I could imagine how he felt about it. I felt very bad about it, too, and a little responsible for the boy's death. A few days before it happened, the other boys I worked with and I were telling him that we were stealing potatoes every night, which wasn't the truth. I think he went there to prove to us that he could do it, too. The German allowed the body to be taken to the old Jewish cemetery in town for burial. That seemed very strange to me, after what the Germans did with the dead bodies in Skarzysko.

Some people were needed to unload boxcars and the foreman picked two of us. That work was very hard. The open cars were full of iron ore and two men with shovels had to unload them by the end of the day. After work, I could hardly move. I couldn't wait until the end of the week, when I would change to the night shift. The unloading was only done during the day. By now the foreman saw that we could do hard labor; he sent us at night to help make sand forms by the big oven. This wasn't easy either. I had to load sand into wheelbarrows from a sand pile in the corner of the room and push it over to the men who worked on the forms. Well, I guessed, my loafing days were over.

I was still hungry. But at least, if I stayed out of trouble, I didn't have to worry about beatings for no reason at all. Here, we felt more like human beings, as human as one could feel under these circumstances. We didn't see any Germans. Occasionally, a Ukrainian guard would walk by, but he didn't seem to bother anyone.

I still played my little game with Jarmolf. It wasn't as interesting as it had been earlier. I think he'd become used to my visits. He looked like he felt safe and content. He just worked in the factory and minded his own business.

The winter was nearly over and the snow gave way to mud. In most places, one could drown in it. It was very hard to walk anywhere outside. A lot of people were put to work clearing the rails. It was tedious, standing ankle-deep in mud with a shovel. Looking back, it wasn't too bad compared to some other duties.

CHAPTER XIV

This day started the same as any other. The daytime shift went to work and since I was on the night shift, I lay down on my bunk and went to sleep. I always came from work so tired, that I could almost go to sleep before getting into my bunk. Pushing wheelbarrows full of sand made me exhausted.

I don't know how long I had been asleep when someone screaming awakened me.

"Get up! Get up! Everyone outside. The camp is being evacuated."

Still half asleep, I didn't realize what was happening. So I went to the door to see what was going on. A lot of men were lined up by the gates, ready to go. Fully awakened by this, I hurried to put on my jacket, grab my soup container and run outside to line up with the others.

The Jewish commandant and his policemen counted us. There were still a few people missing. The policemen ran from one barracks to another to get them assembled. I noticed three Ukrainian guards standing at the gate, looking nervous as they talked to each other. Finally, everyone was accounted for, but we were waiting for the day shift to come back from the factory. As we stood there, people asked each other questions.

"Where are they going to take us? What's going to happen to us," they wondered. No one knew for sure. Someone said that the Russians were very close and the Germans were going to take us to Germany. Maybe so, but one never knew with the Germans. They were full of surprises. They might take us all to be killed. That thought stayed in my mind and made me nervous, too. We had heard that there were concentration camps in Germany, but why would they take us to Germany when they had shipped the Jews away from there to Poland? Nothing made sense. Anyway, I was not alone in feeling nervous. If it's true that the Russians were coming, I could see why the Ukrainian guards would be nervous. I was sure the Russians would like to get their hands on them.

Finally, the day shift arrived and was counted very quickly, then out the gate we went. The guards were very anxious and urged everyone to walk faster. It appeared that they would just as soon leave us and run to save their own hides. Someone commented that we were headed for the railroad station. It seemed strange, since other people were walking around freely in the streets.

I hadn't seen a town in years, and it made me feel homesick and lonely. I wish they hadn't taken us through a town. I wished I could cry, but I wouldn't let myself do it. It was depressing. I began wondering if I was going to be locked up in a camp for the rest of my life. It looked that way.

A thought came to my mind. It would be easy just to jump in a doorway and save myself. If the Russians were so close, maybe I could hide somewhere for a day or so, and wait for them, then be liberated. On the other hand, I couldn't trust the Polish people. They hated the Jews, too. No, I'd better not take that chance. What will be, will be.

We were in the open and could see the railroad station up ahead. We also heard artillery fire not too far away. Maybe we still had a chance. The guards were running, screaming at everyone to run. For a fleeting moment, I thought we should stop right here and overpower the guards, then wait for the Russians to come. It would be easy. But no one would do that so we kept running and running, away from freedom. Well, maybe it wouldn't have worked anyhow. What did I know? I was just a kid.

There was a long train close to the station. Passenger cars were in the front and closed freight cars behind. A lot of people were trying to get on board. There were Germans, many in uniform, with their families. They all looked frightened, men, women and children. They were paying no attention to us. For the first time, I saw Germans who were frightened. What a switch! It must be true that the Russians were very close behind us. It made me feel good to see

Germans on the run, for a change.

As we reached the freight cars, the guards started pushing and shoving everyone inside. While I waited to hop on, I noticed the last car of the train had a flat top with a big artillery gun, and a lot of German soldiers around it. It looked like they had been firing the gun up to the time they pulled into the station. They were now securing it.

We were packed like sardines inside the cars, about seventy people per car. The door was closed and locked from the outside. It was very dark since there were only two small windows in the car, located too high for me to see out of them. If we were going any distance at all, it would be a rough trip. It was stuffy and had very little air in the car, but we all settled down as well as we could. Some had to stand, some sat.

As we moved out of the station, we heard more artillery fire, and even machine gun shots. Apparently, we missed the Russians by only a few minutes, since the sounds were very near. Why didn't we try to escape? Just a few minutes more and we would have been free. How unfair!

As the train moved along picking up speed, we followed our own unspoken rules, taking turns standing and sitting. The train moved along at higher and higher speeds. Wherever we were going and why, would remain a question that was unanswered. A few of the taller men who were with us could see out the small windows and gave us commentary on the scenery and our location.

The air was getting worse. It was stifling. There was a bucket in the corner for those who had to relieve themselves. The smell was becoming unbearable. They hadn't given us any food before we left. I hadn't eaten since the night before and I was very hungry. I wondered when I'd see food again.

The train seemed to speed up for awhile and then slow down, off and on. We began falling all over each other. We felt like cattle being shipped to slaughter. It was getting worse with each mile. The light outside the small windows was dimming.

The train kept moving in the night. Someone said we were in Germany. Surely we were. We'd been traveling for hours and all that time I did not take my turn at sitting. Finally, I asked the man sitting next to me if I could sit. He stood up and I collapsed onto the floor, which wasn't very comfortable. There was no straw, just a bare wooden floor. The train was shaking and jerking, so sitting wasn't much better than standing. But I finally fell asleep, with all sorts of thoughts churning in my mind.

When I woke up, I could see light coming through the window. I must have slept all night. All this time, I was sitting with my legs tucked against my chest. By this time I was so stiff and numb I could barely stand up without falling. The odors were more intense by now, since the bucket in the corner had overflowed. I was glad I was not next to it, but I felt I was going to throw up.

My stomach was making funny noises. I was starving and thirsty. A few hours later the train came to a stop. One of the men by the window said we were at a station. After a while the train started moving slowly, then backed up and stopped. I assumed they were dropping us off because I could hear the train uncoupling, then completely stopping.

After a little while, a Ukrainian guard opened the door slightly and told us we could empty the pail. A man grabbed the bucket and went outside with it, leaving the door wide open so we could breathe some fresh air. One of the men asked the guard when we were going to get some food and water. He replied that we weren't getting anything until we reached our destination. When some asked where we were going, the guard answered that we would soon find out. I didn't like the way he said that. And I wasn't alone with that opinion. The guard slammed the door shut.

After about a thirty-minute wait, a new engine was attached to the train and we were moving again. We traveled through villages and towns but no one knew where we were. Darkness set in again as we continued to move at a steady speed. Where were they taking us? The guard said we would soon find out. What did that mean? When, where, why? No answers, just questions!

The fear of the unknown is very intense, scary. Everyone in the boxcar looked worried. Tempers were flaring; people were ready to fight for no reason, other than fear. This was one of the ways the Germans broke people's spirit: put them together in cramped quarters without food or water, and in time they were ready to kill each other. Put a Jew in charge of other Jews, threaten him, and he will also kill to survive. Yes, it is a matter of survival, but what cruel philosophy. We were like experimental rats are to a scientist.

Some people fainted and fell to the floor, and no one cared. Maybe some of them were already dead. When would we get to where we were going? The hunger pains were powerful and the thirst was even worse. People were tearing into each other like animals. Fights broke out all through the boxcars.

"God! Please stop this insanity," I mumbled.

Another night came. I was still standing up. I must have fallen asleep standing, because when I looked up, I could see light. Another day had passed and we were still moving very fast. How long has it been? I lost track. Two days, three days, a week, forever? I was losing track of time and felt if it went on much longer, I'd go insane. How did it feel to go crazy? Maybe I already had. I felt very weak and faint. Others looked like they were in a trance.

Time passed. I no longer knew how much time, but it must be midday by now! The train was still moving. Things were much quieter in the boxcar. No one had the strength to argue or fight any more. The only sound was the clattering of the train wheels. How much longer? I asked myself over and over again, how much longer, how much longer before we all die.

Late in the afternoon, the train slowed down, then stopped. Everyone came back to life. Where were we? Several men struggled to take a look out the small window.

"We are here! We are here! We are here," they began shouting. They didn't know where, but they could see SS men lined up along the side of the train with clubs in their hands. Their dogs were barking, fiercely welcoming us to our destination. One of the SS men opened the door.

"Everybody out!" he ordered. The dogs kept barking, showing their fangs. Although frightened, we obeyed and jumped down out of the boxcar where we had been imprisoned for days. I looked around. It looked like we were outside another concentration camp.

CHAPTER XV

"Line up, you lazy Jew pigs," the guards screamed at us. They sicked the dogs on us. After we lined up, we were marched a short distance to a big gate. It said WORK MAKES LIFE SWEET. The irony was that they had made me a slave for four years, and now they tell me that work makes life sweet. Maybe my work made life sweet for them, but not for me!

I'd heard of Buchenwald. Talk gets around. A lot of people lost their lives there over the years. At first, it was supposed to have been a camp for political prisoners, but later on Jews and Germans were in, and people from all over Europe. They were in several different compounds.

As we went through the gates, the SS men screamed at us to walk fast. The people were so weak they could hardly walk, never mind walk fast. We stumbled along as some fell to the ground and were bitten by the German Shepherd dogs.

We marched up to the big barracks where the SS men halted the column and told us to line up in single file and enter one by one. As I stood waiting to go inside, I noticed another barracks behind the one we were entering. It had a huge tall brick chimney at one end. I concluded that it must be the crematorium I had heard so much about. Later I found out that the front of that barracks housed a gas chamber. Close to the top of the chimney was a sign that read THE ONLY WAY OUT OF THIS CAMP IS THROUGH THE CHIMNEY. My interpretation of this was that no one left this camp alive. How encouraging! Now it was merely a matter of time before it would be the end of the road for me. I had come a long way to end up here. Four years of misery. Four years of fighting to stay alive, and this was going to be the final struggle.

Why? Why did I fight so hard for this? It made no sense at all.

Inside the barracks there was a big desk at one side of the room. Four SS men were seated behind it, each one with a typewriter, asking the same questions, name, age and birthplace. When I answered the SS man, he told me to go next door. There was another room and another desk with two SS men behind it, ordering everyone to put all their belongings on the desk. Then they ordered us to take off all of our clothing. They examined our bodies to see if anyone had hidden anything of value on their person.

When that was done, we were sent into the next room, which was empty except for a big steel container in the middle, filled with some kind of solution. We were told to get into this container and submerge. A SS man stood there with a club and if someone didn't submerge, he prodded them with it. When I got in, I felt a burning sensation all over my body.

"All the way," the SS man growled. I dunked my head under for a second and then jumped out. My eyes were burning, even though I had closed them as I submerged. My skin felt like it was on fire. The next room had showers that I stood under for a long time. It felt so good to have water on my body. There was no soap, but at least the water washed off that solution that must have been a very strong disinfectant.

After the shower, there was still another room, with a big pile of uniforms for us to wear. They looked like pajamas. Each jacket had yellow patches with numbers on the front and back of it. I searched through the pile to find one that fit me halfway decent. The one I finally chose was too large, but I rolled up the cuffs a few times and it was all right. The uniforms weren't new. I wondered who had worn mine and if he or she was dead while wearing it.

The SS men registered the number of each uniform, and then we were to find a pair of shoes. They were not sorted in pairs, but piled in a corner, in mixed sizes. They were wooden shoes, but that was all right. I had become used to them in camp B. As soon as we had what we needed, the SS men sent us outside again to join other men who were already waiting. Another SS man then counted us. He divided us into groups of twenty, then marched us out, separating us to different compounds. There were French prisoners of war and

Americans. I could identify them by the uniforms they had arrived in. The Gypsies' uniforms were the same as ours, easily identified.

As we came near the Jewish compound, we saw they looked worse that the other groups. The Walking Dead, I thought. If someone asked them their names, I doubted they could respond. I guessed that Jews received special treatment here in this camp.

The guard marched us into a large barracks equipped with three-tier bunks on either side. One could lay down on them, but not sit – no headroom. There were two long tables with benches in the middle of the room. It was hard to move around because of the number of people packed in the barracks. Observing the faces of those around me, I wondered if their expressions were of boredom, sadness, fear, or all of those.

The overseer stayed in a small cubicle in the center of the room. The guard outside called to him and said he had twenty more people. Then he handed him a list of them, by number, not by name. I could see that I had now lost my name; I was just a number also.

A political prisoner was among us. He had a red patch instead of yellow. He was a communist. Compared to everyone else, he looked very good, very healthy. I was told later that he had been in this camp from its very beginning. That was a long time, He must have been treated well to remain this healthy. They said he was a bricklayer by trade, and appeared to be in his early forties. He seemed to be a decent man and didn't bother anyone.

Right outside the overseer's cubicle, there was a chair next to a bed where the assistant overseer stayed. He was a man in his fifties who was once a high-ranking Russian officer. He also seemed like a decent man who, as a prisoner of war, had been here since 1941.

In the camp the overseer was called a Kapo. He told us to find ourselves a bunk and that the soup would be here within an hour and that bread would be distributed later. With all the activities that were going on, I had forgotten how hungry I was, but with the mention of food, I felt I was starving again. When the food arrived, there was a scramble to line up. There must have been a hundred of us in the barracks. I sat down at the table to 'feast' on this putrid liquid they called soup. Well, at least it was hot, and with nothing else to eat, I considered it delicious. Since I had not eaten for three days, I had to enjoy every spoonful. And I had something to look forward to: the bread would come later in the evening.

I looked around the barracks to try to find a few people that I knew from camp B in Skarzysko. I didn't know if we were all on the same train. They came from the munitions factory and told me that there were many people from camp B, but in other barracks. I decided to explore the compound. I went to the next barracks and found it was as full as the one I was in. I found three boys about my age from camp B. They were so glad to see me and, of course, the feeling was mutual. While we were exchanging verbal notes, two young men approached us. They greeted us warmly and said they had been here a long time. They were Russian Jews.

"By the way," one said to me, "do you know any Jewish police-men or commandants from the camps that you came from?" We indicated no, by shaking our heads.

"Now, if you do know of anybody, all you have to do is point them out to us and we will take care of them." I wondered who these young men were. Perhaps a hit squad? Then I remembered the ex-police chief from camp B. I knew he came here with us on the train, but I hadn't seen him at all. The young men wished us good luck and moved along. I watched them as they stopped by another group of men to talk.

After that, they left. Then I told my friends about Jarmolof. They were amused by my story of how I had silently tortured him.

"Boy, you must have driven him crazy," one of them said. "But you were always good at that. I remember the German lady boss at camp B. You smiled at her all the time, too." We all laughed as we remem-bered. Then we said goodbye and promised to meet the next day.

I returned to my barracks, and just in time. Our Kapo was dis-tributing our ration of bread. I got my portion, sat down at the table and began to eat very slowly, as if it were a special occasion I didn't want to end. I was careful not to drop one little crumb. This was only one thin slice of bread. I thought how wonderful it would have been to have had a whole loaf of bread to eat until I couldn't eat anymore. I would be full and satisfied for a change. Well, no such luck! It was only a daydream. I will never be able to do that as long as I live. I will never get out of here.

As I was doing my daydreaming, the assistant Kapo sat down next to me. He smiled at me and asked me my name, how old I was and where I came from. After I told him, he told me his story. He was from Moscow, an engineer by trade before the war. He had worked in a big tractor factory. He married and his wife couldn't have children. They were going to adopt a child, but the war broke out and he had to join the Red Army because he was in the reserves.

He seemed to enjoy talking to me, especially when I told him about my father being in the Russian army during the first World War, and my mother being from Russia. He told me not to worry, that the war would soon be over and that the Russian Red Army would liberate us. I didn't feel very optimistic, even if the Russians or any other army was around the corner, the Germans would manage to kill all of us before they arrived.

The Russian officer told me about the closest town to this camp, by the name of Weimar. The allies bombed it and there was nothing left but rubble. He said the SS took so many men from this camp into town every day to clear the ruins; otherwise, there was no work in this camp any more.

The Germans had built a rifle factory in the middle of this camp and the inmates had worked there but, about a year ago, the Americans precision-bombed and flattened it to the ground. Nothing else was hit, just the factory. No barracks, no nothing. That's precision bombing. Since that happened, no one has worked in the factory.

If no one had been working in this camp, they couldn't be dying from overwork, but they were still dying. Why? What was the problem? Was it boredom, malnutrition, or what was it? Why are they walking around like zombies? They might as well be dead, I thought. Perhaps they just didn't care enough to lie down and be counted.

Practically every day there was someone hanging on the electrified barbed wire fence. It was obvious that those people got tired of their existence and ended it by flinging themselves onto the fence. Every morning, dead bodies were dragged out of the barracks. The way they had us living, maybe the Germans felt that if they left us alone we might die by ourselves. Then they wouldn't have to lift a finger except to pile up the bodies of those who had despaired.

The Germans came into the compound twice a day with their dogs and lined everyone up to be counted. I wondered what it was with them. Were they afraid someone would escape from here? There was the electric barbed wire fence, and if someone got through it, there were two other fences around the perimeter of the camp. Maybe they counted us every day so they would know how many of us had died, and they could tell how much food they saved.

We stood outside while the Kapo and an SS man counted and re-counted. When they realized that someone was missing, the SS men searched for that person or persons. If it wasn't that someone was dead, but only one of the Walking Dead, the person would be dragged outside and thrown to the dogs.

The morning after I came to this camp, I had the experience of watching one of these gory scenes. We had been standing outside for about half an hour when the barracks door opened and two SS men dragged out a man and threw him on the ground in front of us.

The man looked half-dead already. Another SS man unleashed the dogs. Growling and barking, they pounced on the man and tore him apart. When they were through, there was nothing left but a pile of bloody bones.

The SS men appeared to be enjoying the spectacle. They let the dogs attack until the dogs themselves stopped due to lack of interest or hunger. After the dogs had finished their feast, the SS men nonchalantly leashed them and left the compound. I was stunned and felt like throwing up. I had never seen such a gruesome thing in my life, even though I thought I had already seen everything. The hangings, beatings, shooting, etc. were terrible, but this was the most revolting thing I had ever witnessed. I did throw up!

One evening while we were standing outside while the SS men were searching the barracks for a missing person, a woman I had never seen before came into the compound with the SS men and their dogs. I asked the man next to me if he knew who she was. He answered that she was called the bitch of Buchenwald.

"Who?" I asked.

"She is the wife of the commandant of the camp, Madam Koch. Her favorite hobby was finding all of the prisoners with lots of tattoos on their bodies. She has the man killed and then grafts the skins of the body and makes lampshades out of it," he said.

Chills went through me. No, I couldn't believe the story. What kind of person could do something like that? No, it can't be true. But later, my friend, the Russian officer, told me that it was true. He would know since he had been here a long time. He would not lie to me.

I watched this strange lady as the SS men brought a man out who apparently overslept. They unleashed four dogs, which jumped on the man and knocked him down to the ground and started tearing him apart. Madam Koch became excited and seemed to really enjoy this whole horrible scene. The screams of pain from the man who was being chewed while alive and then killed by the dogs, pierced my heart like a knife. I tried covering my ears with my hands, but it didn't do any good. I could still hear the man. Then suddenly it was quiet. I removed my hands from my ears. He was dead! There were no more struggles, no more challenges for the dogs. They were finished with their prey. The dogs were leashed and the SS men walked away, laughing and joking with the woman. What makes a person become a monster, I wondered.

The following day I went to see my friends in the next barracks. They were outside. We began talking about the camp when a man moved over near us. It was Jarmolof. He looked terrible, obviously recently beaten up.

"Look what they have done to me," he moaned, "I hurt all over. They told me I had a choice; I could hang myself or they would kill me. You kids can help me. You can tell them to leave me alone."

"Drop dead!" one of the boys told him. Jarmolof was crying now. Another boy spit on the ground in front of him. I gave him my sarcastic smile, and we all walked away from him.

The next day I heard that Jarmolof hanged himself during the night, with a piece of rope that someone gave him. I felt good about it. I knew in my heart he would meet a bad end, and I didn't have to lift a finger against him. Justice was done. I didn't feel that I had my revenge, but rather that the man deserved the punishment he bestowed upon himself. My conscience was clear.

The next time I saw my friends, I asked them who put the finger on Jarmolof. They laughed as they told me they didn't know what in the hell I was talking about. I had a feeling that one or all of them did it, but I wasn't going to worry about it. Jarmolof wasn't the only one who met with such an end. Policemen and commandants from other camps met with similar fates. I heard that the young men had told the Jewish commandant from camp A in Skarzayako, after two days of beatings, to tell the Germans that he wanted to go to the gas chamber. The SS men accommodated him.

There was no work here, even after two months. People were dying, probably from hunger and boredom. People cannot live without purpose, without hope. If not for my talks every night with my friend, the Russian officer, I would not last long myself. He gave me hope and the desire to live, something to look forward to. He asked me to go to Russia with him after the war because he wanted to adopt me. This sounded very good to me at the time and made me feel great. Someone really cared what happened to me. But in the back of my mind, I felt we would never come out of this alive.

Every day I saw more and more of the men who came here with me turning into the Walking Dead, even though we had been here only two months. How fast a person can let himself go! I guessed all one had to do was lose the desire to live, and the hunger and boredom did the rest. With no purpose, no desire, what's left? It hurt me to see what was happening to these people. They had endured so much, and then to end like this! Some of these men had seen their entire families destroyed all at once, their wives, their children. But they had plugged along. Now they give up? It didn't make sense. On the other hand, nothing was making sense any more. I was fifteen years old, and had been through so much since the beginning of the war I hadn't grown an inch. I was still the little shrimp that I was when I was eleven.

On Sundays in the barracks, the German Kapo called everyone to gather around him. He got up on the bench in the middle of the room and began his speech. He spoke about the end of the war and the glories of the Russian Red Army, and how they were going to liberate us. He spoke of the world revolution and the workers' utopia that would follow. It was a long speech. Every Sunday he said the same things.

At first, it sounded so good that people applauded him, but now it sounded like a broken record and everyone was bored with it. I personally thought he had been here too long and he was not only trying to convince himself, but was trying to keep his sanity. At least he was a good man and didn't bother anyone. Some of the other Kapos were also German prisoners, but they were real bastards and not any better than the SS men. Some were murderers, rapists or criminals of another sort that the Nazis didn't dare put in the SS ranks. They killed people at the slightest provocation.

I thought the Germans took us from Poland and brought us here to Germany because they needed the labor force. But I must have been mistaken. There were thousands of men in this camp and no work. The only reason I could think of was that the Germans didn't want to leave any Jews alive in Europe. Why? I remembered what my father told me. It seemed so long ago: We are the chosen people.

Is this what God wants? Are all of the Jews going to heaven after they are murdered by the Nazis or die from hunger or other reasons?

All these things were going through my mind again. I had so many questions, but no answers. Sometimes I had to tell myself to stop thinking so much, or I would drive myself crazy, but sometimes I couldn't help myself. I wondered if my family was in heaven. Was their pain and suffering worth it? Were they together again? Oh God, where are you?

Life went on in camp. Everyone seemed to be anticipating something that was going to happen, including me. We didn't know what we were waiting for, maybe death, maybe liberation. I didn't know.

One day it happened. The German Kapo called everyone to attention.

"The numbers I will call will go outside," he said. I knew my number by heart. He called fifty numbers, and mine was one of them. I didn't know if it was good or bad to be called. What's going to happen?

Cautiously, I stepped outside and looked over the group already assembled. By experience I knew enough not to rush into anything.

The group here was all men from camp C in Skarzysko. Could they be taking us to work somewhere? Sure enough! The Kapo came out of the barracks and told us he was taking us to the admin-

istration building where we would wait for the SS men, who would
be taking us to a different camp for work.

When we got to the administration building, there were more
men from camp C waiting. The last time the men from camp C
were taken to work, it was to the steel mill. I wondered where it
would be this time. Another factory where the work was just as
bad? Well, it would be good to get out of here, although I would
miss my friend, the Russian officer. Would I ever see him again?

There were about two hundred of us. When the SS men were
done counting, they marched us out of the camp. As we passed the
crematorium, I looked up at the chimney sign that said THE
ONLY WAY OUT OF THIS CAMP IS THROUGH THE
CHIMNEY. I thought to myself, aha, I fooled you! I'm leaving
this stinking camp under my own power and I'm still alive. That
made me feel good.

The SS men marched us back to the station where a train waited. I wondered if it was the same train that brought us here. They
loaded us into three enclosed boxcars and locked the doors. Where
were they taking the cattle this time? The train was a long one, but
we didn't know what was in the other cars. Whatever it was, it had
been loaded before we arrived. As soon as our men were loaded, we
took off.

Again, the fear of the unknown took over. We tried to get as
comfortable as possible under the conditions. I wondered how long
this trip would take. How long would we be without food?
Apparently, the Germans felt that cattle didn't have to be fed when
being transported. I should be used to it by now. We traveled the
whole day, and darkness was setting in. The train stopped at various stations and, when it did, we expected to be at our destination,
but all they did was uncouple a few boxcars or add others. We were
locked in and no one bothered with us.

It was the same at night. The train stopped and started. I finally fell asleep, and when I woke up it was morning. Around midday the train stopped at a station and someone read the sign:
Leipzig. Another man explained that it was a large industrial city in
Germany. We stayed put for quite a while, then the train moved
slowly for about a half hour, then pulled into a factory.

CHAPTER XVI

The boxcar door was unlocked and opened. Three SS guards shouted for everyone to get out. It seemed that they never talked; they screamed or, at least, shouted. We lined up outside the train and they started counting us. Apparently the Germans liked to count. They spent most of their time doing it. What did they think? Someone might have escaped through those little windows you couldn't even put your head through? We were marched toward a big factory that was three stories high, up the stairway and to the third floor. There were two large rooms with bunks lined up three tiers high. The room housed three German Kapos. We were told we could choose bunks on one side of the room. People who were at work occupied the opposite side of the room.

Before long, the men workers appeared. To my amazement, they spoke strange languages. Some spoke Yiddish, some were Hungarian Jews. They told us they had only been there for one month and that this was their first experience at a camp. The Germans had just begun eliminating Jews from Hungary. These people looked good, well nourished. Even though they wore pajama-like uniforms (the same as ours), somehow they were different than the Polish Jews. They spoke their native language and sounded like they were always arguing in loud voices. I found out later that most of them could not be trusted, not all of them, but most of them. They would even inform on each other for special favors from the Germans. They would call each other 'Magiars,' which in their culture meant thieving Gypsies.

In each of the two big rooms on this floor was a small room where the German Kapo lived. In our room, the Kapo was a young-looking German prisoner, a homosexual who had a young

Hungarian companion who stayed with him in his room.

We were in Colditz, just a few miles from Leipzig. There were quite a few different camps. One had Poles, Russians, French and British prisoners of war. It was situated in a castle on a mountain overlooking the factory.

The morning after we arrived, the Kapos escorted us down to the second floor. The SS men met us and ,again, counted heads. Everyone would work in the factory; however, he or she would select three of the younger boys to work in the kitchen. A SS man asked me how old I was. Of course I lied and told him I was thirteen. Why not, I didn't even look thirteen, more like twelve. He picked me, and I got to work in the kitchen. I decided I probably would like it there. The Kapo led me to the kitchen along with two Hungarian boys. We followed him gladly!

The cook was a Polish man who had Polish helpers. He put us to work peeling potatoes. There were tons of potatoes. (I thought back to when I was almost killed for stealing a small bucketful.) The task was difficult for me at first but, when I got the knack of it, it became easy. The cook wasn't very friendly, and neither were the two other helpers. But, when the soup was done, he would save extra portions for us.

It didn't take me long to figure out how to steal some potatoes. Every day the same men came in from the factory to pick up containers of soup for the workers. One night I talked to the two men and we agreed that I would slip some potatoes to them when they came in for their containers of soup and, later, we would split 'the take' three ways. I didn't dare take any myself because every so often the Kapos searched us on the way out of the kitchen. It worked pretty well. Every night I had a few potatoes to eat. I cut them up in slices and stuck them on the chimney of the stove that sat in the middle of the room. When one side was done, I peeled it, then stuck the other side to the chimney – like fried potatoes!

The men working in the factory told us that they were working on some unknown gadgets. Some thought they were parts for V1 and V2 flying bombs that the Germans flew over England. No one knew for sure.

During the day and at night, the allies were bombing the city of

Leipzig. In the daytime hours, air raid alarms sounded every few hours. When they went off, we could see the terror on the faces and in the eyes of the Germans as they ran for shelter in the basement of the factory. They encouraged workers to do the same. I couldn't help thinking as I saw the fear and terror in the eyes of the Germans that perhaps if they were half human, they would understand the fright and panic they inflicted on us and have some compassion. Everyone went to the shelter during the day, as ordered. At night when the alarm sounded, and the Kapos screamed for everyone to get up and go down to the shelters, no one went. We stayed in our bunks. I guess it was a mutual feeling among the Jews that it was better to die by the bomb of the ally than a German bullet or the gas chamber.

At night, we knew that the Americans were doing all the bombing. I had become quite an expert. I could tell by the sound of the plane exactly who it was, American, British, or Russian. The Americans had the biggest bombers, the British second and the Russians had the smallest. I rested well at night, knowing that the Americans didn't give the Germans any rest at all. It may sound funny, but lying there in my bunk, listening to the alarm going off, I was excited when I would hear the roar of the oncoming American planes overhead. They came in waves and dropped lanterns that lit the city until it looked like daytime outside. Then came the whistling of the bombs being dropped until they hit their target, followed by tremendous explosions. It was strange, but I no longer had fear, but rather a kind of satisfied feeling that the war was coming to an end. If only I could have the chance to enjoy the end of it with my family! How I missed them.

There was no German opposition to the bombing. The allies came, dropped their bombs, and left. Where was the German Luftwaffe? Didn't they have any planes left? Only sporadically could I hear the anti-aircraft fire. Didn't they have any guns left either? I speculated that perhaps the Germans were running out of ammunition. We slaves had all been transported from the camp where we had made the German's ammunition. In any event, they couldn't hold on too much longer with all this continuous bombing.

I felt that the end of the war was coming and there was no question that Germany would go down in defeat. The question still remained as to what the Germans were going to do with us Jews. Would they let us go or would they kill us? I thought the latter.

After we had been working for a month in the kitchen, one of the SS men entered the kitchen and announced that he was taking two of us boys into town where we were needed to do some cleaning up. I was one of the two he selected. Outside, there were another twenty men waiting. The familiar counting took place, after which we were paraded to the gate and out onto the road.

The town of Colditz was small and apparently had been hit by bombs the night before this. Many buildings were in ruins. We were put to work by the SS men to clear the debris. We were warned not to talk to the civilians, who looked at us as if we were some kind of dangerous criminals. We couldn't talk to them. They probably were told that we had leprosy.

From the looks we were getting from the German civilians, and their attitudes, I began to feel like we WERE what we were being called: Jew pigs. But that didn't last very long; I got used to it. Besides, I consoled myself with the thought that they were getting a taste of their own medicine. How do you like your glorious Third Reich now? How do you like your Fuhrer who brought you to this? And this was only the beginning! I hoped the next time planes came they wouldn't leave one building standing. I wished I could have stood on a soapbox and shouted this out to them in contempt of everything they stood for.

While we worked, I noticed a young German boy, not more than ten years old. He wore short black velvet pants, long knee socks, and a brown jacket with a swastika on the sleeve. I had seen these boys before in Poland. They were the 'Hitler Ugen' (Youth of Hitler's regime). The youth approached the SS man who was propped up against the debris of a bombed out building and thrust his arm out in the Nazi salute.

"Heil Hitler," he shouted. The SS man haphazardly lifted his arm and answered,

"Heil Hitler." The boy asked him if we were Jewish. The SS man said yes.

"I will make them work faster," the youth said.

"Go ahead," the disinterested SS man said. Appearing encouraged, the youth picked up a club off the ground and started hitting us one by one.

"Hurry up you dirty Jews! Move faster, move faster, Hurry up!" he screamed. Watching and showing approval, onlookers smiled. The SS man looked bored and, as long as the boy was enjoying himself, be never said a word, I wanted to grab this boy by the throat, take the club, and shove it up his ass. This was a perfect example of how the Jews were seen through the eyes of the Germans. What could you expect from Hitler's Nazi Ugen?

It was humiliating! How much more of this would we have to take? The civilians were gathering in groups, sneering. Some were laughing out loud. I wished I were dead. The only consolation was that I was clearing the destruction done by our allies. Yes, I would blot out everything else except that thought. It helped. I had just resigned myself to all of this when the boy got tired of playing his game with our lives and left. Good riddance!

At lunchtime, the SS man took us back to the factory and said he would pick us up after lunch, in the front yard of the factory. I tried to think of some way to get back to my old job in the kitchen, but I was afraid he might come looking for me. So, after lunch I went back to town with the rest of the group. The rest of the day was uneventful. That night, the SS man told us to report tomorrow to the same spot. This was going to be our job until it was done. Well there went my easy job in the kitchen, right down the drain! We would be cleaning up this town for a long time. But I knew that the more we had to clean, the more discomfort there was to the Germans. The bombings continued day and night.

When the siren went off during the day while we were working, the Germans started running in a panic to the shelter in the middle of town. Our SS guard urged us to run fast and took us to the same shelter with the other Germans. It was located in the big basement of the Ratthause, the City Hall. The guard kept us separated from the German civilians because we might contaminate them – the leprosy, you know. We had to listen to the snide remarks some Germans made about us, especially the ones from the women. They said things like how terrible it was that they must stay here with the dirty Jews who fouled up the air they breathe, how filthy the Jews were, and things like that. I wanted to tell those women exactly what I thought of them, but I didn't open my mouth.

Our SS guard ignored the remarks. I guess he agreed with them, but he had to guard us and he wasn't about to stand outside while the bombing was going on. Most of the bombs were falling in Leipzig, but it was so close to Colditz that it sounded like they were falling right outside City Hall. When they sounded the All Clear signal, we all went back to work.

We had been working in town about a month, and still no end in sight. Every so often we heard artillery fire, which meant only one thing, the front was coming closer and the end of the war was imminent. But would the Germans allow us to live? That remained to be seen.

One day it happened. That morning the Kapos told us that no one would go to work, which made us all very nervous. What was happening now? What ere they going to do with us? Here we were again overshadowed by the fear of the unknown.

Late in the afternoon, the Kapos told us to assemble in the hall-way. The German commandant and three SS guards were waiting patiently for us, which was very unusual. When everyone had gathered in the hallway, he began to speak. This, too, was very unusual. The Germans always screamed or at least shouted. He told us how well we had performed our duties for the Third Reich and, for us, the war was going to end tomorrow, that the Americans were going to take over the camp.

There was a moment of absolute silence. Can you imagine what those words meant to all of us? Then a spontaneous, thunderous yell came out from everyone. The commandant was still speaking, but no one heard him. No one was listening! This time, we were screaming in delight, hugging each other and, in general, it was pandemonium!

The commandant, frustrated and overwhelmed by the celebration, retreated with his guards. The celebration continued late into the night, until the people were so tired, they reluctantly went to their bunks and went to sleep, in spite of their excitement and expectations. I couldn't sleep, with all this going on. What would it be like, being liberated, being freed? How would the Americans treat us?

So the local Germans were going to get their wish. I overheard them talking among themselves when we were working in town, saying that if the war was lost, they didn't want to fall into the hands of the Russians, who they were deathly afraid of. Apparently they knew what the German army did to the Russians while in Russia. Now they were afraid the Russians would take revenge on the German people. My thought was that it couldn't happen to a 'nicer' people.

As I lay in my bed, unable to sleep, I noticed an unusual calm in the air. No bombing tonight; no artillery fire. It was as if the world was standing still. Were the Americans here already? Maybe the Americans weren't coming at all, and the commandant was tricking us into believing we would be liberated, and they would kill us all tomorrow. I was frightened. My mind kept going over all the possibilities. Some were positive, some negative. Just before morning, I finally fell asleep.

I woke up to some of the excitement and merriment of the night before. People were talking and laughing, but mostly just waiting for the Americans; then beginning to wonder what was holding them up. The morning went by, and nothing happened. No Americans, nothing! We did not get soup at noon, but on one was thinking about food. We were just waiting for liberation, which wasn't coming.

Later in the afternoon, the SS guards, with rifles drawn, walked into the room and started screaming at everyone to go down to the courtyard. The once jubilant people became frightened and uncertain. Cautiously, we went outside. There were a dozen SS guards with rifles drawn, ready to shoot. I sensed that something wasn't right. It had been too good to be true. After all, we should have known we couldn't trust the Germans. What were they going to do with us? Were they going to kill us now, when we were so close to being liberated?

SS Guards came out of the building, full packs on their backs. That probably meant they were going to kill us first, then go to the front to fight. We soon found out what it meant.

"We are evacuating the camp and you are going to go on foot this time," the SS commandant said. "Each of you will get a half loaf of bread. Eat it sparingly, because I don't know when you will eat again."

As we stood there waiting, the SS men got the Russians, the Poles, and Frenchmen from their camps. I guess we were all going together. We formed a long line and the Kapos gave out the bread. A half loaf of bread! That was more bread than I'd had all at one time in years. After everyone was given their bread ration, the gates were opened and the whole column marched out of the factory compound.

CHAPTER XVII

There were guards at the front, rear and side of the column. At first, everyone walked quite swiftly and briskly, but soon the column began to spread out, as people grew tired. Initially, we were walking segregated from the Poles, the Russians, and French; but the farther we walked, the more mingled we became.

It was getting dark, but we kept going. Were we going to walk all night? Maybe the SS men had a destination for us to reach by tonight? We wondered.

We were led off the main road onto a road in a thick forest. Soon we came to a clearing and the guards instructed us to stop. This was where we would be spending the night. As the moon became visible through the trees, the guards began taking their positions around the clearing while most of us fell to the ground, exhausted.

When we received our ration of bread that morning, I noticed that the Russians ate their entire portion as soon as they got it, but the Jews, knowing better, were eating theirs one piece at a time, conserving most of it for another day.

I sat down on the damp, cold grass. There were no blankets or other covers. Since all I was wearing was the thin pajama uniform, I didn't want to lie down and get wet. I got up and wandered around between groups of people who were falling asleep. The night soon became a scene of terror, a nightmare. The Russians formed bands and began attacking the Jews. They knew the Jews still had most of their bread rations, so the Russians decided to steal it from them. Seeing what was transpiring, I ate the good-sized piece I had, rather than give it to the Russians. They were behaving like animals.

All night long I could hear screaming coming from all directions.

I was very frightened. I stayed on my feet in the dark. When the dawn came, I sat down and fell asleep. When I woke up, most of the people were already standing. I must have lain down while sleeping, because I was wet from top to bottom. My teeth chattered as I lifted myself from the ground. Although it was spring, it was very cold.

The SS men went around and found a few Jews still lying on the ground, so they began kicking them. There was no response. Russians who were looking for bread had stabbed five Jews to death. The SS men told us to fall in line. We then marched out of the woods, back to the main road, leaving the dead bodies in the forest.

Our escorting SS guards looked older than those we had encountered before. One would imagine that the Germans musts have been scraping the bottom of the barrel to have these older men on this duty. As we walked, I tried to inch my way forward to the front of the column. I wanted to be the first one to get wherever we were going.

We walked for several hours before we were allowed a rest stop. No, it wasn't really to give us a rest; I believe it was because the guards were tired. We rested for fifteen minutes, and it was almost enough time for everyone to catch up. At the end of the column there was an elderly SS man. He was tall and slender and looked frightening. He must have been a boxer in his younger days. His broad nose was flattened to one side of his face. The skin beneath his eyebrows looked like it had been scarred many times. He had 'cauliflower' ears. He had a mean look on his face, or maybe he just had a mean-looking face. I couldn't decide.

The signal was given at the end of the rest period for everyone to get up and start walking again. It had felt good to sit and rest for a while, but getting up again was another matter. My legs felt like two pieces of lead. I was still young, but having a hard time. What must it have been like for others who were much older than I was. After I walked a little while, it became a bit easier.

The lieutenant was leading the group, followed by two SS men. One was middle-aged, and the other was an older man who looked like he was really laboring with his backpack and rifle. Watching him gave me an idea. What if I asked him if I could carry his backpack? It looked like we were never going to get any food, so, if I helped him, he might share some of his food with me. He must have some in his backpack. No, bad idea! I could hardly walk myself, how was I going to carry his pack? Maybe I could try. He looked like a good-natured man, not at all like the SS guard. I'll wait until we stop for a rest, I thought, then I will ask him.

Late in the afternoon, we started up a little hill. Glancing back, I saw people stretched out for a mile. Some were walking slower and slower. At the top of the hill there was a roadblock, a barricade across the road. Some youngsters and a few old men stopped our column. They looked funny, wearing uniforms that didn't fit and holding rifles of the First World War vintage. A few of the young boys could hardly lift the weapons. I speculated again: is this what's left to defend Germany, their Fatherland?

They told the lieutenant in charge of us that we couldn't go any farther. The Americans were coming this way. The lieutenant had us turn around and head back the way we came. That was fine with me. It was easier going downhill. We soon caught up with the people who were still walking in the other direction. They were dragging their feet like they would collapse any minute. Some did. They told us that the old guard in the back of the column was shooting those who couldn't walk anymore. On the way downhill, I counted twenty-one bodies lying in the ditches on either side of the road. Was I going to end up there, too?

We took another road. I wondered if the guards knew where they were going. Finally, they did let us rest again. I went over to the older guard as I had planned and asked if I could carry his backpack. He looked me over, up and down.

"You can hardly carry yourself. How are you going to carry my backpack?" he asked with a smile.

"I'm all right," I said, "and would like to try."

"Okay," he said, holding a faint smile, "Then I will give you some bread next time we stop for a rest."

When we started up again, he helped me get his backpack on. It was so heavy, I wondered how far I could make it with it on my back. But I kept on walking with the guard, and every so often, he looked at me. A couple of times, he even asked if I was all right.

The farther I walked, the easier it got.

After a few hours, they signaled to stop. I sat down next to my guard who helped me remove the pack from my back. My shoulders were sore from the straps but, otherwise, I was okay. Unpacking his bread and cheese, the guard carefully cut two very thin slices of each and gave me my share. I would have been happy with a thin slice of bread, but cheese too? I couldn't remember the last time I saw a piece of cheese, let alone a piece I could eat. I was so hungry that my reward for carrying the backpack made the load seem lighter. I ate ever so slowly, but when I finished I was just as hungry as before. But I knew it would keep me alive for quite a while.

The guard was very friendly toward me. We talked and he told me he didn't want to be in the SS For that matter, he didn't want to be in the military at all. One day, the SS men entered his shop and took him away. Without any training, they gave him a uniform and a rifle and sent him to this camp to be a guard. He also told me that the night the commandant made the speech about the Americans coming to take over the camp, he was telling the truth. Unfortunately, that very same night the American president, Roosevelt, died and in his honor the American high command gave an order to cease-fire for the next twenty-four hours. Therefore, the commandant got orders to evacuate the camp. When I asked him where we were going, he said he didn't know.

"I don't ask questions," he added. "That way I stay out of trouble. The only thing I know is that we are going a long, long way."

With the backpack secure on my back, we started on the next lap of our journey. What lousy luck! The president couldn't die a few days later? We would all be free by now. Who knew how many more men were going to die before this was over? Two thousand men had left the camp. There were mixed nationalities. It was mostly the Hungarian Jews who couldn't walk anymore. Obviously, they weren't used to hardship. They had been taken from their homes only a few months ago. We Polish Jews had been through hell for almost five years and, so far, most of us had taken everything that the Germans could dish out. Now, I wasn't too sure. The best of us were weakening, due mostly to starvation. If the guard was right, that we were going a long, long way, I was afraid that not too many of us were going to make it.

Every so often, a car pulled up in front. Next to the driver sat the camp commandant. They talked for a while, then drove off. Apparently, the commandant was asking the lieutenant instructions as to which way to go. They must know by now where they were taking us.

Toward evening, it looked like we were approaching a town. There were buildings in the distance. Before we reached the town, the lieutenant took us into a big field. When everyone was gathered, the lieutenant told us we were free, and that the Americans should be here very soon.

Again, there was instant excitement. Everyone started dancing, embracing each other, and jumping up and down. To look at them, you would never have known that just minutes earlier, they were barely alive. We went through this same thing not too long ago. Was it for real this time? Should I get excited? I was leery, so I stood back and watched one of the guards being beaten by some of the Russians. Another guard ran into a clump of trees and changed into civilian clothes that he had in his backpack. I gave back the backpack to my guard.

"I better make myself scarce, and good luck to you," he said. I thanked him and wished him good luck also. No sooner did I say that than I saw the commandant's car speeding toward us. He started screaming at his guard to assemble, and they talked for a few minutes. The lieutenant then took his revolver and fired a shot into the air.

"Okay, all you bastards, fall in," he shouted.

I knew it! I knew it was too good to be true. The excitement was gone. The crowd grew quiet, and they all fell in, as commanded. In a split second, a bunch of Russians started to run toward some distant trees. The lieutenant gave the order to the guard to shoot. The Russians scattered, but some of them fell as they were shot. A few escaped. The Germans didn't bother to go to see if they were dead or merely wounded. They just assumed that if they fell, they were dead. Maybe it was too late to care.

The next word from the lieutenant was "march," so we marched.

The small town we marched through looked completely deserted. There wasn't a living soul to be seen but, somehow, I had the feeling we were being watched by the inhabitants from behind drawn shades. We passed from one end of town to the other, in the dark, onto another road. I wondered if they would have us walk all night long. A few miles out of town, we were led to another open field, where we would spend the night. I fell down onto the grass, not caring if it was wet or dry. As I lay there, my thoughts wandered. What rotten luck! This was the second time we had been foiled. I felt we were never going to be freed.

That night, I wasn't afraid to close my eyes and sleep. No one had any food, so there was no reason for the Russians to attack. How long could we exist without food? I was better off than the rest. At least, I had had a piece of bread and some cheese. That brought me little satisfaction at this moment. I was starving!

The next morning, we continued on for the third day. How much farther? The column was moving slower and slower. By now, we were stretched out for a couple of miles. When they let us stop for our fifteen-minute break, we were ready to start up again before the last man caught up. The guard at the back would urge them along with his pistol. Some were able to drag themselves along, but some just lay there. With that, the guard merely walked over to them and shot them with his pistol. One man, barely alive, begged to rest for just a little while. But bang! He was dead. What a bastard! I hoped one day that the German would burn in hell, if there was such a place. There obviously was no God, or He wouldn't have allowed all these atrocities to occur, in spite of what my father had kept telling me. So if there was no God, there was no hell after life.

We were living in our hell right here.

By midday, we were approaching the big city of Dresden. We were about two miles outside it, but we could see it as plain as if we were at the city limits. All I could think of was being able to rest when we got there.

Suddenly, there was a siren coming from the city. The lieutenant screamed for everyone to hit the ditch, but not in time. The planes were overhead. A car with four soldiers passed. Three of them looked like officers. We jumped in the ditch and counted six planes approaching the city, flying low. One broke away from the others and flew directly above us. It was flying so low that I could see the pilot. He tipped the wings of his plane first to one side, then the other, as if he was saying 'hello' to us. There was a bright red star on each wing. They were Russians!

The plane flew directly over the car in front of us and sprayed it with bullets. The car veered to one side and flipped over in a ditch. He must have gotten them all, because they were not moving. As we lay in the ditch, we watched the planes diving and dropping bombs. Some buildings crumbled and others exploded. As fast as they came and did their job, they left.

When we entered the city of Dresden, we found nothing but ruins. There didn't appear to be one building left standing in one piece. People looked dazed as they ran around in the streets. My, my, what happened to their cozy little nests, their safe and secure existence! This was their first encounter with the war their beloved Fuhrer started. How did it feel? No different, I'm sure, than when your glorious armies and the Luftwaffe destroyed the homelands of other Europeans. We walked onto the open road again.

Later that afternoon, we came upon a small town. When we reached the center, the commandant was waiting for us in his car. He directed us to a farm on the outskirts of town. The farm had a concrete wall around it with double steel gates at the entry. Each gate had solid steel plates on the bottom and iron bars on top, to deter anyone from looking outside, but also no one could look in from the outside.

They marched us inside the gates, which were then locked. On one side of the large courtyard stood the farmer's house. In the back were two big barns where we would be staying overnight. Shortly thereafter, the SS men brought out two buckets full of potatoes boiled with skins on them. When we lined up, each of us was given two potatoes. That was not adequate for people who hadn't eaten for days, but at least it was something.

A crowd of Germans gathered outside the gate. Standing on their tiptoes they watched us, like animals in a zoo. I was standing near the gate when an older woman who was watching us called me over to ask what kind of crime I had committed. Apparently the SS men told the people we were dangerous criminals. I told her that I murdered my whole family. She darted away in a panic.

"Such a young boy. Such a young boy," she muttered.

Night came and everyone entered the barn to sleep. It was warm and full of straw. For a change, we all slept well and felt rested the next morning. The SS men told us to fall in, and he counted heads. Someone must have been missing, since the guards began searching the barns. Soon they came out with a man who had overslept. The SS lieutenant hit him in the face with his fist and the man fell to the ground. The lieutenant proceeded to kick him with his heavy boots.

The man cried and pleaded with the German to let him go, but the lieutenant shot him in the head. Why? I guess to the Germans, oversleeping was a crime, too.

We left the farm and were back on the road again for a day of marching. How much farther? We ran into another roadblock and turned around again. It seemed like we were walking in circles. The guard who brought up the rear was killing more and more people.

It seemed like the bastard really enjoyed killing people. One time when they allowed us to rest, the guard brought a man up front with him. He asked the lieutenant to lend him a bullet. The lieutenant obliged. The guard put the bullet in his revolver, walked over to the man he had brought with him and shot him.

I hoped the old guard's legs would give out on him; maybe the other guards would shoot him! If this killing continued, there wouldn't be anyone left when we reached our destination. Two thousand of us had started this march, and I don't believe there were more than six hundred left at this point.

I heard someone say that we were getting close to the Czechoslovakian border. That made sense. They wanted to get us out of Germany. It would be much easier to shoot us and get rid of us that way. I guess the German minds didn't work that way. It would be too easy for us. They must first make us suffer to the point where we begged to die, and then they would shoot us.

We kept on walking while others were getting shot. The day was coming to an end. Off in the distance, I could see another village. The commandant in his car led us toward another farm. They again put us up for the night. The only difference was that there was no food. I was so hungry I could have eaten a horse, but there was no horse.

I recalled the Walking Dead from the other camps. That's the way they all started. The hunger got so bad that they lost their minds and simply gave up. I wondered if I would become like that.

Where and when will all this end? I fell asleep that night wondering if that would be my last day on earth. I was so hungry and tired I doubted that I could last another day. My legs were numb; my feet were like two pieces of lead. My stomach felt like it was tied in knots.

The following morning I woke up without the sound of screaming and shouting. The sun was rather high in the sky. It must have been nine or ten o'clock. Something must have been wrong. Usually, we were awake at the crack of dawn. What's happening, we all wondered.

There was a well in the middle of the farmyard. I pumped it a few times and splashed the running water on my face and took a drink. I felt a little better, a little refreshed. Even my legs felt better.

Finally, the guards came and began counting heads. Two were missing. The search turned up two dead bodies that had been left in the farmyard. The farmer would have to dispose of them. As we left the village, I asked my guard if I could carry his backpack again. He asked if I thought I was strong enough.

"I'm fine. I think I could walk forever," I lied. He smiled and gave me his pack.

This was our fifth day of walking. A few miles down the road we entered Czechoslovakia. The countryside looked the same as Germany. In the first village, the residents were standing outside. Men, women, and children cried openly when they saw us go by. These people knew we weren't criminals.

On the other side of the village we stopped for a rest, which I welcomed. The backpack I was carrying was getting heavier and heavier. After I dropped the pack near the guard, he opened it and pulled out a small bag from which he took a half dozen boiled potatoes. He gave me one, and told me that this was all he had left to eat. The bread and cheese were gone.

"The potato is just fine," I said. At least it was something I could put in my stomach.

"You know, the commandant had a meeting with the guards this morning," he said. "He asked us if we want to continue on to our destination. If not, we would have to take all of you into the forest and kill everyone. A couple of the others and I were against it, but most of them wanted to do it and get it over with. However, when the commandant told them that if they didn't want to continue on, we would all be sent to the front to fight. They all agreed to go on at that point."

Then, I understood why they were so late getting to us this morning. Before we started up again, the guard told me to try to hang on, that it wouldn't be too far now, maybe another day or so. Well, that was encouraging. I only hoped that my legs wouldn't give out on me. I was glad all the Germans weren't the same. My guard was a very nice man. I was sure he didn't like doing this, but he must or face being shot himself.

As the walk continued, men were dying left and right. That guard in the back was having a good time shooting these poor people. I somehow stayed up front and kept telling myself to keep going.

"Keep going," I said to myself, "you can't stop now. It's just a little farther. My friend, the guard said so and I believe him. He is a good man. Keep going!"

I hoped my legs were listening to my thoughts and mumbled words. When I fell back for a while, I caught myself and started walking faster until I got back to the front of the column. I began talking to myself again. "Keep going. You don't want to die here. But where are we going? To another concentration camp? If and when we get there, what then? Will the Germans leave us alone? Will they let us live? Maybe the gas chambers were waiting for us to arrive. Wouldn't that be something? If I survived this death march, only to die in the gas chambers! Well, at least I am alive today. Keep going!"

We were nearing the end of another day and at this time, we were nowhere near a village or town. When it got dark, the guards placed us in an open field. I collapsed to the ground like everyone else, and fell sound asleep. By morning, I was so stiff I could barely get myself up from the ground.

It was the sixth day and we were on our way. Our sixth day, and no food. I have already had a few potatoes from the guard, but the others had nothing. I wondered how they could keep going. Were they stronger than I was? I guess it was just their will to live, just as it was with me. We always hoped for a better tomorrow. But this was yesterday's tomorrow, and what would happen? Who is going to make it through the day?

They have separated the Russians, Poles, and the French from us Jews. Are they going to some other place? Now I could really see how few of us were left. Most of the Hungarians were gone. When we left the camp, there were five hundred of us Jews and now there were less than one hundred. I didn't know how many Russians, Poles and French were left, but when they separated us, there were not very many.

The whole morning I kept telling myself, don't stop. Keep going. It will soon be over. We will soon be 'there.' Don't stop.

Later that afternoon, we finally reached our destination: Terezinstadt.

CHAPTER XVIII

Terezinstadt was an old fortress, surrounded completely by a twenty-foot-high stone wall. An old stone building with grass growing on top of it was built in as part of the wall. There were openings in the wall where cannons had been positioned at one time. Beyond the wall, there was a town with paved streets, sidewalks and buildings with stores, all surrounding a very neat square with trees and flowers. All of the buildings were brick, in keeping with the old architectural style.

Our guards led us to the gates where two Czech policemen stood on watch. I said goodbye to my friend, the guard, who wished me good luck. His job with the Jews was finished, and he would be going to the front. The police opened the gate and let us in.

As we all gathered inside the gate, we were counted by the SS men again. Then we were marched away from the entry. As I looked around, I couldn't believe my eyes! This neat town had all German Jew residents. There were older people sitting on benches in the square. There was an outside café, a bank, and a town hall. I didn't find out until later what this was all about. The Germans used Terezinstadt as a model city.

Whenever the International Red Cross inquired about the Jews, the Germans would bring them here and show them how humanely they were treating the Jews. However, what was not shown to the Red Cross was that once a month, a transport with people would be going to Auschwitz for extermination. The Germans then brought new people into the city to replace the others.

The old people here now were the lucky ones. And there were some people with small children. This was the mixed group the Germans kept for show. There was even Jewish money (printed by the Germans) which, of course, wasn't worth the paper it was print-ed on. This was the sham, utilized to show what great people the Germans were and how well their prisoners were being treated. If only the world knew the truth!

The guards marched us to a large apartment building with a bal-cony on the second floor. Gates led onto a courtyard, guarded by two Czech policemen. There were many people out on the bal-conies, Polish and Hungarian Jews, who were brought long before us from various concentration camps.

The guard took us inside the building and down to the cellar. It was more like a dungeon. In fact, it was a dungeon with cells, dark and damp. We were locked in the cells, along with some others who had been there for a few days. We learned they were all brought here from another camp. They were luckier than our group. A train had brought them here.

I asked one man if they had been getting any food and he said we could be thankful for that.

"In fact," he continued, "the soup should be coming any time now." The ration was one bowl of soup per day, no bread. The only way to think of this was that it was better than nothing to eat.

Soon the door opened and a Jewish man brought a container of soup. While an SS guard stood in the doorway. The soup was watery and tasteless, but it was hot and stopped the hunger for a while, the extreme hunger we had felt for the past week.

The only light in the room came through the steel-barred win-dow up above. Looking outside, all we could see was a sidewalk. At night it was chilling. Why were they keeping us down here? Some people were on the street, some locked in their rooms upstairs, and we were in the dungeons. Why? What did the Germans have in store for us now?

It had been three days since we were placed in the dungeon. On the fourth day, an SS guard took us upstairs to the second floor where there were big rooms with cots. At least, we would not have to sleep on the dirt floors while there. There were a lot of people from Germany here. Quite a few of the men were sick; dysentery had broken out a few days earlier.

I learned that this building was once a barracks for soldiers and, before the war, the Czech army used this whole town as a boot camp. The dungeons were used as a prison for army offenders. Now, the SS was using it as a torture chamber. We had been put down there for quarantine. Everyone who came here recently had to spend a few days down in the dungeons.

I explored the building to find out where I could hide, in case I had to. I couldn't see any escape from here. Every window had steel bars. Every room was big and open. There were even over-sized bathrooms (which were not in working order due to the dysentery that had broken out).

More and more people were getting sick each day. The SS men didn't bother us much. When someone would die, they took the body outside and put it in one corner of the balcony. Although the pile of bodies was getting bigger each day, no one seemed to notice. If we stayed here much longer, everyone would be getting the sickness.

While peering out the windows, we could see people walking around the grounds, carefree, as if there were no war. What a contrast! Why were we being kept locked up? It had been over a week and nothing had happened. There was a tension in the air, as if something was about to happen, but no one seemed to know what. The end of the war? Liberation? Death? Whatever it was, all we could do was wait. Nothing was changing. The food was the same, and by now we were all used to being hungry.

People were talking about the end of the war. It must be near. Any day now, we would be liberated. The front must be very close. I didn't hear guns. The allies must be concentrating on Germany. Who knows when they would come here? And when they did, would it be too late? I was becoming such a pessimist. But no wonder! I have seen so many times that we would have been free, but then something always happened.

Two weeks had gone by since we entered this place. I couldn't even walk into the bathrooms. There must have been two inches of shit on the floor, spilling out into the corridor, and no one did anything about it. The smell was atrocious.

More people got sick. More people were dying. It seemed there would be no end to it.

"God, if you do exist, why don't you do something for these poor people," I cried to myself. "Why? Why do you allow this suffering? It's not fair. But then, the whole stinking war is unfair."

We waited. Every minute was like an hour, and the agony continued. My appetite had left me. The endless waiting, the fear and uncertainty of what was coming taunted me. I felt sure they would kill all of us just before the liberation. It was very tempting to go out onto the balcony and scream at the Germans to come and get us and get it over with. Yet, I kept telling myself that where there is life, there is hope.

CHAPTER XVIX

There was nothing unusual about this day. I got up and washed my face in the sink in the hallway. Suddenly, I heard a shot coming from out in the street. After running back to my room, I saw other men already looking out the window to see what was happening. A man screamed out from between the iron bars.

"The Russians are here."

Then a Russian shot his gun into the air and ordered the Czech policemen to open the gate. With that, we all crowded onto the balcony to get a better look. A Jeep with two Russians, a driver and an officer, was entering the courtyard. When the vehicle stopped, the officer jumped out and looked up at the people on the balcony.

"You are free! You are free!, he shouted. All that could be heard at that time were screams of joy. People ran into the courtyard from all parts of the building. I didn't know what to do or feel. I had been through this before, only to have the dream shattered. However, an ally had never before announced it to us.

People swarmed onto the courtyard and hoisted the officer and driver up on their shoulders and carried them around the yard. It seemed strange, because an hour earlier these people could hardly lift themselves from their cots. The strength must have been coming as a result of the newfound hope. The officer, with tears in his eyes kept repeating, "You are free. You are free. You poor souls, you are free." The people were half crying, half laughing. Their happiness was beyond description.

At last, the people finally lowered the two Russians back to the ground.

"You are free, free to go wherever you want," the officer again told us. "The Russian army is on the highway outside of town. If you want to go see them, that would be nice." With that, he stepped into the Jeep and slowly pulled out of the courtyard. This time it was really true. We were free. I wished I could go home to my family. That would make a perfect ending to the hell I'd been through.

All of us followed the Jeep into the street and onto the highway. By the time I reached the spot where the Russian equipment (trucks, tanks, and Jeeps) were parked, many people were already lined up to get on board. We crawled, stepped and jumped into the vehicles, and as we drove through the center, people cheered the victorious army. The soldiers joined in the jubilation by waving and throwing things to the people: whatever they had, such as cigarettes, bread and other items. The whole scene was overwhelming in joy and celebration.

We saw German prisoners walking down the road. By the time they passed me, they had already been beaten and stripped of their belongings by the ex-prisoners who were welcoming the Russian army.

I couldn't help feeling sorry for some of the Germans. Some of them might not be deserving of this kind of treatment. But neither was I. In some ways, it made me feel a satisfaction to see them run and cry like little children. I had seen most of the same soldiers in the glory time of the Third Reich, arrogant and pitiless. This was my revenge for the mistreatment, the beatings, the starvation, the humiliations, all of that.

The Russians didn't stop the attacks on the German prisoners. They just looked and laughed. The Russians must have approved of the treatment the Germans were getting. I couldn't blame them for feeling that way. They knew of the atrocities inflicted by the Germans on defenseless people. For what the Germans did in Russian, these German soldiers weren't paying too high a price.

When the crowd caught a SS man, they didn't let him get away. Most of them were beaten to death. I saw one of them on the ground with four knives sticking in his body. Then I thought of the guard who let me carry his backpack. He was a good man. I hoped he was all right.

Later in the afternoon, I went back to the town. The kitchen was open and anyone could get as much soup as he wanted. In all the excitement, I had forgotten I was hungry. Next to the kitchen there was a large dining room where I sat down to eat. The soup was good this time. I even had bread along with it. I surprised myself and only ate one portion of soup and bread. I was full. I thought that surely I could eat much more.

I watched others devouring their food. That was not good. Our stomachs had shrunk so much that those people would be sick if they continued to gorge. They could even die from eating too much at this time. And so it was. During the next few days after our liberation, more people got sick and more died of dysentery. What a shameful waste! To go through all we had endured, this whole nightmare, and then to die of overeating. Almost unbelievable.

After my meal, I returned to the building where I have been staying. It was evening, and I was exhausted from the events of the day. I would go to bed for the first time in years as a free man. That was a wonderful feeling.

When I got to the second floor, there was a big commotion in front of the washrooms. Some of the men had whisked away two SS men from the highway right under the noses of the Russians. They then brought them here to have 'fun' with them. The SS men were tall, young and blond. They looked like the ones who volunteered at the beginning of the war for Hitler's elite group. The men pushed the Germans into the toilets and told them to clean them with their bare hands.

It was a pathetic scene. Two young supermen from the master race, standing there, crying like small children, shoveling shit with their bare hands. I had to feel sorry for them. No one should get punished like that. Besides, I felt that if we did to them the same as they did to us, then we were no better than they were. Revenge was not sweet to me. I just hoped that justice would prevail. I wanted the allies to seek out all of the Nazis after the war and put them on trial, and handle the punishment in accord with the laws.

The two SS men pleaded with the men who were making them do that revolting job. They claimed they had been forced into the SS ranks, and that they had only been fighting for a short time. They begged the men not to kill them. I couldn't watch any more, and walked away in disgust.

I lay down on my cot and tried to sleep amid the noise. The men were reviewing the events of the day, and it seemed like none of us would get any sleep that night. The latest story they were discussing was that the German commandant had been building gas chambers and a crematorium, and had orders to eliminate all the Jews. Everything was ready to start, but he realized that the war was lost and he wanted to save his own hide.

He had contacted the International Red Cross and told them that if they would give him safe passage to Switzerland, he would tell them the secret. They agreed. The Red Cross contacted the Russian High Command. The Russians had plans to take Prague, the capitol of Czechoslavakia but, instead, they made a detour and took our camp first. This was what saved our lives.

For most of the night, I couldn't rest or sleep even though I was very tired. When I finally did fall sleep, I had a nightmare. The Germans were chasing me. I was running, but couldn't get away. I woke up in a cold sweat, fell asleep, but had a repeat of the nightmare, over and over again. Would I continue to have these nightmares? Would I ever be able to sleep peacefully? Why not? The war was over!

The following morning, the moaning and groaning of the sick people in the room woke me up. Some had died already. Not knowing what to make of it all, I left the building and went out into the street. I felt nervous walking in the street. I was not used to being free. Then I began watching the Russian soldiers, still on their march. One of them tossed a candy bar to me as I waved to them. I hadn't seen a candy bar since before the war, five years ago. I had forgotten how delicious they were. In the afternoon, I went to the kitchen. There were dumplings in the soup. I had forgotten what they tasted like as well. The dumplings were a Czech delicacy. I was able to eat a little more on that day than I had the day before.

Later in the afternoon, the Russians brought in a truck full of nurses. They carried the sick in their arms and took them into the hospital, which had been set up in a building on the edge of town. Along with the nurses, a team of doctors arrived. They were all trying their best to serve the sick. As I watched this, I was thinking what wonderful people, the Russians!

On the next day, they set up a place for delousing. They took our clothes and burned them. After we were bathed and disinfected, they gave us some drab but clean clothes and shoes. For the first time in years, I was wearing underwear and socks. Slowly, I was beginning to feel like a human being again.

A few days after the liberation, the Russians started a registration. All the kids up to the age of fifteen were being taken to a children's home. I was nearly sixteen, but I lied about my age, and I was admitted to the orphan's home. For five years I hadn't grown an inch, so I had no trouble passing as a fifteen-year-old.

There were two hundred of us in the home, boys and girls, in separate quarters. A doctor examined each of us. The majority of the children had something wrong with them, mostly in their lungs. A couple boys were diagnosed as having TB. I was given a clean bill of health and almost felt guilty because so many of the sick ones were getting packages from the United States with all kinds of good things like fresh oranges, canned goods and powdered milk. I didn't get anything. That was the price of being healthy!

After a week in the children's home, I started getting depressed. Now that I was free and didn't have to worry daily about being killed, I started thinking about other things. Here I was, sixteen years old and my whole family was gone. I was free but all alone, with no one to turn to. Where would I go? What would I do? The reality was that I would have to shift for myself, just to stay alive. Prior to this, I always had orders to follow. My miserable life had been controlled at all times. But now it would be different. The Russian's chant 'YOU ARE FREE' echoed in my mind. But I asked myself: where do you go when you are free? How do I decide where to go and what to do? I knew there was a big world out there, but my thoughts were plagued by confusion.

I fell into a melancholy state. I lay on my cot, day and night, staring at the ceiling, scared. I couldn't focus on any particular thing. I didn't even want to eat. My friends tried to force some food into me, but I fought them.

"I don't want to eat," I would scream at them. But a few times they held me down and forced soup in my mouth.

Finally, my friends called one of the Russian doctors, who examined me. He could find nothing physically wrong with me and told my friends that I would snap out of it eventually. Later, my friends told me that I had been like that for two weeks. That was after I got out of bed and asked them when the food would come.

"I'm starving," I told them. I believe I was in a deep sleep and finally awakened, completely refreshed. Then I was all right.

Outside, I found a different environment, a whole new administration. The soldiers weren't very friendly. The women were afraid to be alone, not only at night, but when walking the streets day or night. They complained to the authorities about being raped by the soldiers, but all they were given was a deaf ear. Sometimes, they were scolded by the Russian commandant for enticing the soldiers.

The soldiers stole anything and everything they wanted, and looked like they were drunk all the time. Many times I saw them sitting in a circle with a bucket of water, a slab of raw bacon and a loaf of bread. They passed these among themselves to feast on. It was hard to believe that these were the same kind, considerate, compassionate army men who had liberated us. Now, they were turning into animals.

I noticed machinery on open boxcars being shipped to Russia from all over Czechoslovakia. That meant that the Czech factories were being dismantled and, piece by piece, shipped to Russia. The Czechs would have to rebuild a whole new industry. That's the price they were paying for liberation from the Germans.

Agents from Poland and Hungary were sent to coax the Jews to return to their native lands. I listened to the Polish agent and decided not to go back to Poland. Many Jews did return, including a few of the children. I did not want to go back because I had too many sad memories and, besides that, I had no one to return to.

A couple weeks later, two of the boys who left for Poland, returned with stories about what was happening to the Jews who went back to their native lands. The Poles wouldn't give back the property that the Jews had owned before they were forced to leave. In order to keep the property, the Poles trumped up phony charges against the Jewish owners, stating that a cow was stolen in town and the Jews did it. They even incited a mob that called for the death of the Jews.

The Jews were being forced to flee their hometown in the darkness of night. If they were caught (and some were), they lost their lives. The Poles dreamt up many false charges. Another charge was that a Jew had kidnapped a small child. Jews were lucky if they could even find their own property, let alone find a small child to kidnap. I wondered why the Polish government was asking the Jews to return to Poland. Perhaps they were going to finish the job Hitler had started.

The Russians began making overtures to us kids. The commandant came to our children's home and gave all kinds of political speeches. He urged us to go to Russia, telling us about the workers' Utopia, about what fantastic opportunities we would have there. There would be free schooling, a choice of jobs, and so on. I don't think any of the kids believed this propaganda. I, for one, didn't. I remember what my father had told me about communism, and because of what I could remember and what I saw going on there, it didn't appeal to me.

People began disappearing, never to be seen again. I heard of a story that happened a few days earlier. A man who came to this town at the same time I did went into a village we had passed when the Germans brought us here. We knew that some of the farmers in this area were Germans, because this part of Czechoslovakia has been called Sudetenland. The Russians looked away when our people robbed the Germans. They found a German Kapo who had been in one of the camps we were in. He was on a farm. They took him out on the road and were going to give him a beating when a Russian spotted them and asked what they were doing. When the men squealed on the Kapo, the Russian pulled out his revolver and shot the Kapo on the spot. If this was the code of ethics of a communist, it was no better than fascism. Therefore, Russia was the last place I would want to go to live.

One day a friend of mine and I sneaked out of town to go to Prague. We had to leave cautiously because the Russians were not allowing anyone to come in or leave without permission. We wanted to see Prague because we had heard it was a beautiful city. We walked to the next town, Laitmerice, and boarded the train to Prague. We had to wait a whole day for the train and when it did arrive, it took three hours to reach Prague in the middle of the night.

We slept for a while during the train ride.

We still wore tags on our lapels, stating which concentration camp we had come from. We took a tram to get to a hotel downtown where some friends of my companion were staying. To our surprise, the conductor wouldn't take any money from us for the ride. When we reached the hotel, we found it was full of people from concentration camps. There was no charge to them or to any of us.

The building was four stories tall. We found a room where six other people were sleeping, so we had to sleep on the floor. That was fine with us. By the next morning, we looked like typical tourists. Yes, the city was beautiful, just like the people who lived there, the Czechs. Wherever we went, whatever we wanted, it was free. No one would take money from us. What a difference between the Czechs and the Poles! We even got to see a free movie.

History tells us that in Czechoslovakia the Jews enjoyed freedom and equality; that during the war the Czechs helped the Jews escape from the Nazis. It must be true. My friend and I spent four great days in Prague.

The city itself escaped destruction, unlike some other big cities in Europe. The allies didn't bomb Prague, and the Russians didn't have much resistance from the Germans when they advanced into Czechoslovakia. But at this time, a political struggle started. The Russians insisted that this country should embrace communism, and they became very adamant about it. The Czechs were always very democratic, but because they were grateful to the Russians, and they really had no choice anyhow, the country became communist. Prominent people began disappearing. Some were said to have committed suicide. But when the truth came out, we learned Russian agents murdered them.

When my friend and I returned from Prague, we were just in time for some good news. In our absence, a Jewish Czech doctor had been in to talk with the kids. He claimed he had connections with the British government, and that they were willing to take us all to England, if we would like to go. We did want to go, but were a little skeptical about it. We weren't sure how influential this doctor actually was, but we hoped he did have the power to do what he claimed. We would go almost anywhere, except to a communist country.

The town was becoming deserted. People were leaving by the trainloads. Many of the Polish Jews were going to western Germany instead of back to Poland. Some wanted to get to Palestine by this route. The Russians didn't like this very much, but they allowed them to go.

My group was getting nervous. We were afraid the Russians wouldn't let us go. The already poor relations between the kids and the Russians were worsening. We were being ignored, and in return, totally ignored the Russians. There were no more speeches from the communist, no fraternizing with the soldiers. Nothing!

The news reached us that Germany had fallen. The war had come to an end. But we were still here. Our doctor came to talk to us again about the negotiations going on between the Russians and the British, to allow us to go to England. The only people left in the town were the Russians and a few Czechs who did the cooking for us. That made us very anxious. Another week passed and we didn't hear a thing about our fate. The town seemed spooky with most of the people gone.

Finally, the day came when the doctor announced that he had reached an agreement and we would all be going to Prague as soon as he could arrange for transportation. After Prague, the British would be sending airplanes to take us the rest of the way. We were all very excited. At last, everyone believed that we would get out of here, leaving behind the last remnants of the concentration camps and the war. To me, it sounded like heaven, but my secret desire was to eventually go to America, the Land of the Free, which I had learned about in school.

Within a few days, four trucks arrived to transport us to Prague. We packed our belongings and piled into the trucks to be driven all the way to Prague. Upon leaving, I felt a chapter of my life had come to an end. I recalled the fear of death I had felt just before the end of the war, the death march that brought me here, the hunger and nightmares of all the concentration camps. For a moment, I felt like an old man, but happy to be alive. I could become young again, dreaming, looking to the future in the strange new land. In England, I would meet new people, learn a new language and adapt to new customs.

Before the day was over, we arrived in Prague, and were taken to the same hotel where my friend and I had gone a short time ago. The following week was unreal. We were treated to movies, concerts, and a visit to a zoo and to a circus. I was alive, and so grateful for the Czech people. I still cannot find words to describe their warmth and friendliness. One lady even got up from her seat on the tram and offered it to me. I declined the offer, but it made me feel so good to be the recipient of such a gesture. It was the same everywhere we went. I began to almost regret leaving this fine country because of the people. I also felt very sad for them because of what the future would hold for them. When the Russians would take over, they would be suffering, even though they did not deserve it.

The day of departure from Prague came. We were told to stay close to the hotel because the planes from England were on their way to pick us up. After we packed, a truck arrived to transport our luggage. Lately, I had little more besides my soup container. About noon, the buses pulled up in front of the hotel to take us to the airport. During the bus ride, we started singing. This was a very happy group of youngsters.

There were six large four-engine bombers waiting for us, the same ones I had watched when they were bombing Germany. Little did I know at the time of the bombing, that some day I would be flying in one of them. As soon as everyone was seated, the planes took off, one right after the other. At that moment, I had mixed emotions. I was sorry to leave this country, but glad to leave behind the dreadful war that had killed six million of my people, including my own family members. The war that had made us all suffer unmercifully, the war that was supposed to end all wars. I asked one question. Why?

EPILOGUE

When we arrived, Jewish organizations, with the help of the English government, put us up in hostels all over England and Scotland. The people were very nice. I learned tailoring, and in 1948 I was married at the age of eighteen. My oldest son was born in England and we lived in London. Even though I liked England, I always wanted to come to the United States.

In my limited education in Poland, which was only six years, I learned about America, the land of the free. Also, America was far away from Europe and very bad memories. Finally, in 1952, we arrived in New York. People even told us that you could find gold in the streets of New York. I hate to tell you what I found in the streets of New York: sweatshops. I worked in sweatshops when we got there, but it was not what I wanted to do for the rest of my life.

So I quit and became an entrepreneur. I drove a cab in New York, which wasn't the most desirable job. After two years and three holdups, I left that job and New York.

I had some friends in Youngstown, Ohio, who had factory and sales offices of pre-cut homes. We moved to Ohio in 1956 and I worked five years for that company in Youngstown, and Pittsburgh, Pennsylvania, and Cincinnati, Ohio. Then, the company promoted me to manage an office in Milwaukee, Wisconsin.

After five years, I started working for a Florida company which was developing land there. That job took me all over the United States bringing people to Florida to buy land. After I was working for a number of years, the company was sold, and since then things were not the same.

So, I quit that job and we moved to Merrill, Wisconsin. My wife and I bought a neighborhood tavern. I became involved in politics, and was elected to the county board and served as president of the business association. After five years, we sold the tavern and dabbled in different business ventures.

Our children moved to Appleton, Wisconsin, and my wife and I followed. I am retired now, but devote most of my time to speaking in schools and different groups. My topic is my experiences during the Holocaust. I feel that the past shouldn't be forgotten because history repeats itself. I love to talk to students and leave them with a message about prejudice and bigotry.

The message is as follows:

I experienced the worst prejudice and bigotry that ever existed in the world, and I can interpret prejudice and bigotry with one word and that is HATE. Why do we hate each other so much? After that dreadful war, in my childish mind, I thought that the world would have learned a lesson and that from then on nations would live in peace and that people would live in harmony, but what a disappointment!

The strife for power, greed and recognition is as strong today as ever before. People are still killing in the name of God. If we believe in one God, why do we hate each other so much. When one hates, that one breaks the very core of human existence. When you hate, you actually hurt yourself more than the one you hate. But when you love, you build bridges between people. When you love, you make a better world not only for yourself, but for everybody in the world. Hate is nothing and love is everything.

Not long ago, a wonderful friend of mine told me that I have a lot of hate in me. At first, I said me? I don't hate anybody and she said yes, you do. I started to think and I realized that I did have a lot of hate and animosities deep down in my heart. But I thought, aren't I entitled to hate what they did to me, what they did to my family and my people? Aren't I entitled to hate? And then I started to think again, and then I forgave.

And when I forgave, I started to love and my whole outlook on life changed. I want to repeat again and again: HATE IS NOTHING AND LOVE IS EVERYTHING.

I speak to students in schools and I tell them my story, not because I want them to feel sorry for me or the people that died.

You can't help them any more. I tell my story to illustrate what one human being is capable of doing to another.

The students are our new generation. Soon they will go into this world on their own and become future leaders, and they can make a difference. If they will remember any part of the story I just told them, they will never allow it to happen again. I feel that another Holocaust can happen to anyone at any time anywhere in the world. White, black, yellow. Man, woman, child. I love you all.

FOOTNOTE: If I can save one child from hating, then my
      effort is worthwhile.

Fill out the form on the reverse side
of this page to order additional copies of Ragdolls.

FOR ADDITIONAL COPIES OF THIS BOOK

Send to:

Name_____

Address_____

City_____State____Zip_____

Cost each: $12.95 plus $3.95 shipping and handling

Number of copies:_____ @ $12.95= $_____

WI residents add 5% sales tax ($.65) $_____

Total $_____

Clip and mail with remittance (check or money order, no cash) made out to:

Henry Golde
2011 Regency Court
Appleton, WI 54915

FOR ADDITIONAL COPIES OF THIS BOOK

Send to:

Name_____

Address_____

City_____State____Zip_____

Cost each: $12.95 plus $3.95 shipping and handling

Number of copies:_____ @ $12.95= $_____

WI residents add 5% sales tax ($.65) $_____

Total $_____

Clip and mail with remittance (check or money order, no cash) made out to:

Henry Golde
2011 Regency Court
Appleton, WI 54915